HYDROPONIC LETTUCE PROI

A Comprehensive, Practical and Scientific Guide to Commercial Hydroponic Lettuce Production

Dr Lynette Morgan

Casper
publications
Pty Ltd

INTRODUCTION

This book is designed to provide detailed information of a practical, scientific and plant physiological nature, for any grower who is currently involved in hydroponic lettuce production or considering producing such a crop. While hydroponic salad crops are often seen as being easier to produce than fruiting crops, such as tomatoes and cucumbers, the degree of skill required to produce a quality product and fully utilise hydroponic technology is still high. The background information about the lettuce plant - physiology, types, nutrition, growth and development - will provide the basis for production techniques which maximise the potential of hydroponics to produce high yielding, good quality salad crops.

ACKNOWLEDGMENTS

I would like to thank Ted Cook of Paraparaumu, Des Dawe of Ohau, Carol and Phil Henderson of Raumati and Otaki Hydroponics whose systems are featured in the photographs of this book.

Graphic Design & Illustration by Leon Wilson
Cover Design by William Chute
Managing Editor - Roger Fox
Printed by Mailing And Print Services Pty Ltd
8 Aquatic Dr, Frenchs Forerst, NSW 2086

Published in 1999 by Casper Publications Pty Ltd (A.C.N. 064 029 303)
PO Box 225 , Narrabeen, NSW 2101 AUSTRALIA
Email: casper@hydroponics.com.au
Internet: http://www.hydroponics.com.au
Printed in AUSTRALIA.

ISBN 0-9586735-2-7

ABOUT THE AUTHORS

Dr Lynette Morgan PhD (Horticultural Science)

Dr Lynette Morgan holds a PhD from Massey University's Plant Science Department in New Zealand, completed in 1996. Her thesis examined many aspects of hydroponic greenhouse tomato production, including investigation into new production systems, nutrition, plant physiology, and the effects of solution EC, environmental conditions and cultivars on fruit growth and flavour. With experience as a commercial hydroponic lettuce grower, and consultant, Dr Morgan is now a partner in 'Suntec Hydroponics' which specialises in hydroponic product development and information transfer. Dr Morgan has also produced a number of specialist articles for high technology publications, such as *Practical Hydroponics and Greenhouses* and *The Growing Edge*. Having been involved in hydroponic growing for over 10 years, Dr Morgan determined that there was a need for a comprehensive publication on crops such as fancy lettuce and other salad greens to be written for commercial growers, and this has been the objective of this book.

Simon Lennard B.Hort.Sc

Simon Lennard holds a Bachelor of Horticultural Science from Massey University, completed in 1990, and has also studied for a Masterate of Plant Science. Simon now runs a large container plant nursery as well as being a partner in 'Suntec Hydroponics', where he specialises in nutrient formulations and system design. His experience on a number of horticultural properties has provided the horticultural engineering knowledge which has been used to provide the system information detailed in Chapter 5.

CONTENTS PAGE

CHAPTER ① - INTRODUCTION

CHAPTER (1) - INTRODUCTION

BACKGROUND AND ORIGIN OF THE LETTUCE PLANT

Lettuce (*Lactuca sativa*) in its various forms, is the most important salad vegetable grown today, but has been cultivated for many centuries. All lettuce originate from the wild species *Lactuca serriola* found in clearings in woods, rocky slopes and waste ground, from Asia and North Africa to northern Europe (*Phillips and Rix, 1993*). It is a winter annual, germinating in autumn, and forming rosettes of leaves which become very conspicuous on roadsides when they begin to flower in late summer, the stems reaching 2 metres in height. Some closely related wild species are found in the mountains of Turkey, Iran and the South Caucasus, and other wild lettuce are native to woods and plains in North America, including *Lactuca canadensis*, sometimes called wild opium.

HISTORY

Lettuce were grown by the Romans, but are thought to have been first cultivated by the ancient Egyptians in around 4500 BC. Wall paintings in some Egyptian tombs are thought to represent a narrowly pointed form of Cos lettuce (*Phillips and Rix, 1993*). The Chinese have grown lettuce crops since the Fifth Century AD, and it was probably introduced into Britain by the Romans, who favoured the plant after it was said to have cured the Emperor Augustus. The earliest post-Roman mention in Britain is in Gerald's Herbal in 1597, where he mentions eight varieties. Seed was later taken to America by the first early settlers. Lettuce with firm hearts are only known with certainty from the Sixteenth Century onwards. Modern breeding has concentrated on resistance to disease and bolting in common types, and on more fancy leaf shapes and colours, such as increasing red intensity and differences in leaf serration and frill.

The heavy, crisp head lettuce grown intensively as a field crop, was developed in America in order to survive transport from California to the markets in the east. Looser, softer cabbage lettuce are more popular in northern Europe. Cos lettuce are widely cultivated in the eastern Mediterranean. In China the Celtuce, a variety with swollen crisp fleshy stalks, is widely grown for use sliced and stir fried.

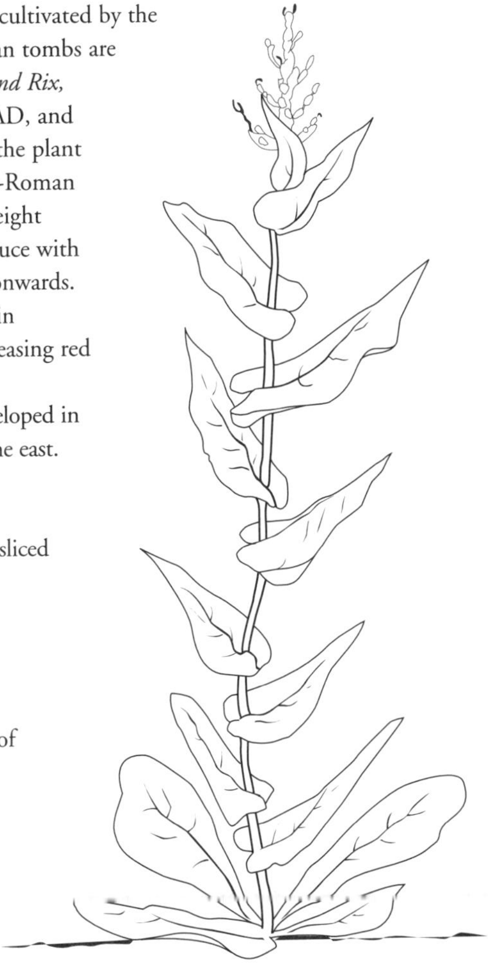

Figure 1. *Wild Lettuce in Flower (Lactuca serriola)*

NEW ZEALAND INDUSTRY

Hydroponic lettuce has been produced in New Zealand for a number of years, but has increased dramatically in popularity during the early 1990's. There is still an increasing number of outdoor lettuce units being installed, while a number of large established greenhouse growers also exist. Many outdoor growers install a simple form of cloche over the individual lettuce tables for crop protection.

The approximate area of hydroponic lettuce produced in New Zealand in NFT (Nutrient Film Technique) is 10 - 20 hectare (1995). The actual size of area in production is difficult to determine, due to the large number of semi-commercial small backyard units in existence. Many growers have well under 1000 square metres (1/4 acre) in production, but there are also a number of quite large operations. These types of systems used in New Zealand are based on those developed in Australia in the early 1980's. Almost all units consist of growing 'tables' or 'benches' which support 6 to 8 small NFT channels. These growing benches are constructed at waist-height and support a plastic or shadecloth covered cloche-frame for crop protection. The NFT channels are constructed from PVC and come in various shapes and sizes, with modifications for fittings and removable lids. Greenhouse growers utilise the same types of gullies as outdoor producers and many also take advantage of the controlled environment to heat the nutrient solution and therefore obtain higher winter production levels. Some growers have automatic pH and conductivity (CF or EC) controllers on their systems, but most smaller producers rely on manual control.

There exists the potential for the development of new, less expensive types of systems to be introduced in New Zealand, but with a large number of systems being sold as 'package deals', this has not occurred to the extent it has in countries such as Australia.

MARKETING OF FRESH LETTUCE IN NEW ZEALAND

Fancy, gourmet lettuce is either sold fresh direct by the grower to restaurants, supermarkets, brokers, caterers and gate sales, or sold through produce markets (no longer auction markets). An increasing quantity of lettuce is being processed for the fast food chains, supermarkets (as salad packs) and for export.

The demand for fresh whole hydroponic lettuce has increased rapidly in the last few years. Not only are catering establishments and restaurants utilising the visual appeal of fancy lettuce as a garnish, but supermarket sales have also been on the rise. For years, New Zealanders' only vision of a salad lettuce was the outdoor grown market garden varieties, i.e Crisp Head lettuce. Today fancy lettuce, particularly the red varieties, are taking a market share.

There are a number of factors which will continue to add to this increase in the popularity of exotic salad vegetables. Firstly New Zealanders, like the rest of the developed nations, are becoming increasingly health conscious. Current campaigns like Vegfed's 'Five Plus a Day' promotion, encouraging New Zealanders to increase their consumption of fresh fruit and vegetables, and point-of-sale advertising has seen an increase in fresh vegetable use. Hydroponic lettuce has the very real advantage of being sold with the root system still intact and sealed in a plastic bag. These 'living lettuce' have an added consumer appeal of keeping longer in good condition once purchased.

Secondly, fresh salads have increased in popularity over the last few years, both for home consumption and as a healthy option for dining out. Finally, more people are eating out, more often, thus restaurants have begun to take advantage of the visual impact of the fancy lettuce types. Upmarket restaurants and Hotels are now looking for food of different colours to add another dimension to the plate. It seems that both New Zealanders and tourists now 'eat with their eyes' as well as their palate.

FRESH-CUT PRODUCE

While the home market is more conservative and less willing to pay premium prices for exotic fruits and vegetables, there has been a trend for supermarkets to stock prepared foods, in particular fresh salad packs. While New Zealand has lagged behind other countries in the sale and use of pre-prepared fresh vegetables, the volume and variety of these packs is increasing. A number of large commercial hydroponic producers and vegetable processors now pack their own brands of fresh salads.

One of the first countries to develop fresh-cut technology was France, where the industry is now well established. There, 20% of fresh consumers are buying fresh-cut products on a regular basis, with most buyers being from the higher and middle income categories. The age group 25 - 50 makes up two thirds of the sales volume. Fresh-cut produce has become big business in the USA, with new products and mixes appearing at the rate of approximately one per week (*Anon, 1995a*). Fresh-cut items are the fastest growing sector in American supermarkets and this component of fresh produce has become so specialised, that it now has its own trade magazine - 'Fresh Cut' - which is published twelve times a year. In Europe, the fastest growing market of fresh cut product is the UK. The quality department store chain Marks and Spencer now sell 90% of their produce as fresh-cut. Holland too is a big consumer of fresh-cut vegetables, 30% in the food service sector such as caterers and restaurants and 70% through retail outlets. The Danish market is similar, with 80% sold to the food service sectors and 20% through retail outlets, however the product range is extensive with items such as white cabbage, grated carrots, and celeriac.

Salad vegetables such as hydroponic lettuce now have their shelf life extended through fresh-cut packaging. Improvements have been made which allow produce to be seen in plastic containers without them fogging up. Modified atmosphere packaging is providing even greater shelf life via the use of vacuum sealing, with carbon dioxide (CO_2) and nitrogen gas injection. Around 10 - 14 days shelf-life can be obtained from salad packs if this latest technology is used during preparation. The technologies involved in producing fresh-cut produce include modified and controlled atmosphere, low temperature, pasteurisation and moisture control.

In New Zealand, pre-packed salads were largely pioneered, but not exclusively so, by the Foodtown chain of supermarkets (*Anon, 1994a*). However, all major supermarkets now stock various brands of fresh-cut produce. Over recent years, the push for pre-cut packs has come from Turners and Growers, who set up what amounts to the factory production of a range of prepared salads and vegetables at the top end of the quality spectrum.

There are a number of salad combinations using the so called 'gourmet' lettuce. Combinations include Red Oak, the frilled Lollo Rossa, smooth and buttery Butter Head, curly Endive, Green Oak, Radicchio and the more familiar Iceberg (Crisp Head) lettuce. Some of these salad vegetables are new to consumers and give people the chance to try a range of the new salad greens without purchasing whole items.

With one source stating that fresh-cut sales could represent 25% of the market by the turn of the century, there exists a huge potential for hydroponic growers to not only produce large volumes of fancy lettuce, but to diversify on a greater scale into the more exotic salad greens. Endive, Radicchio, Chicory, Asian greens and a range of fresh herbs can all be grown in traditional lettuce systems, to take advantage of the latest trends towards pre-packed 'value added' mixtures.

THE AUSTRALIAN INDUSTRY

Hydroponics has allowed the development of many horticultural enterprises in regions that, due to lack of good soil and sufficient water supplies, would not have otherwise been considered for crop production. Last decade, most of the fancy lettuce market in Australia was based on Mignonette and Butter Head types, but over the last 10 years many other lines of fancy salad greens have increased rapidly in acceptance and popularity. Many operations sell

Examples of small 'back-yard' semi-commercial hydroponic lettuce units in New Zealand.

direct to local restaurants or through wholesale agents, however, some large grower networks have been set up in recent years. There are a number of larger growers marketing their own salad mixes, with combinations which include just about every variety of lettuce as well as Radicchio, Rocket, Mizuna, Mibuna, Beetroot leaves, Red Chard, Spinach and edible flowers such as Nasturtiums and Marigolds. Salad mixes are often sold as consumer packs of around 100g, or catering packs of up to 3kg boxes.

CHAPTER ② - THE LETTUCE PLANT
GERMINATION & MEDIA

LETTUCE PROPAGATION - SEED

There are approximately 800 raw seeds per gram of most lettuce varieties, and these can be purchased as 'raw seed' or pellet ('prill') seed. Pelleted seed consists of raw seed, coated with a layer of inert material and clay. As the pellet absorbs water it splits open, allowing immediate access to oxygen for more uniform germination, and better emergence. Some coated seeds are also primed to extend both the temperature range (thermocure treatment) and speed of germination. Lettuce seed pelleting improves the shape, size and uniformity of raw lettuce seed for more accurate seeding and easier handling. The approximate size of most pelleted lettuce seed is 3.25-3.75mm in width.

DORMANCY AND STORAGE

Lettuce seed suffers from 'thermo' dormancy problems, and freshly harvested seed will not germinate at high temperatures until this dormancy is broken. Seed life is usually quoted as being 3 years, but it will often store longer, although some loss of percentage germination will occur as seeds age. Dormancy usually disappears by the time the seed is one year old, but even old seed can become dormant if exposed to high temperatures (above 24°C). Thermal dormancy is a common cause of failure to germinate in summer conditions. The degree of thermal dormancy experienced in a particular seed sowing, is determinate upon variety and seed lot.

Best germination results are obtained from a media temperature of 20°C or lower. The use of coated or pelleted seed is beneficial in warmer conditions, as the pelleting material broadens the temperature range in which the seeds will germinate, overcoming some of a seed lot's thermal dormancy. Seed will germinate in conditions as cool at 3 - 4°C, but all lettuce seed requires light for germination and should be left uncovered, or with only a thin layer of media covering the seed.

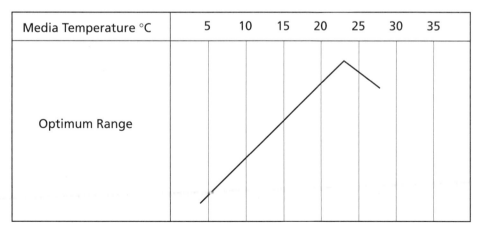

Media Temperature °C	5	10	15	20	25	30	35
Optimum Range							

Figure 2. *Lettuce Seed Germination Guide*

SEED SOWING

Lettuce seeds are usually sown direct into either small propagation blocks, pots or cell trays of inert media. Many larger growers use automatic sowing machines, capable of handling bare lettuce seed. Pelleted seeds are easier to manually handle than raw seed and can be quickly sown by hand. Days to germination can range from 2 - 15 days, depending on growing conditions. Sowing into blocks or individual cells removes the necessity for pricking out, which is a labour intensive operation. The seedlings can be grown and held for 2-3 weeks in individual cells and this also provides the most efficient method of planting out into the hydroponic system.

MEDIA AND SEEDLING PROPAGATION CONTAINERS

Many types of media can be used for seedling production - composted bark, pumice, expanded clay, perlite, vermiculite, oasis, coarse washed river sand, rockwool, expanded plastics and potting mixes. For best results, the media selected has to allow air to reach the roots, and supply the oxygen requirement of the plant. It must also retain sufficient water and nutrient between watering cycles, to keep the plant stress-free and provide support for the seedling. Another important criteria of any media is that it is disease free. Sterile media removes the possibility of crop infection and reduces the requirement for chemical sprays.

SELECTION OF A SEED RAISING MEDIA

Selection of a media for seedling production is based on a number of factors - water holding capacity, aeration, hygiene, ease of handling and cost. While relatively small volumes are required for lettuce seedling production, it is essential that the media provide the right physical properties for rapid seedling development, while nutrition is controlled by application of nutrient solution. It is often a good idea to experiment with a number of different seedling systems, to determine which best suits the growing system being used.

Oasis Blocks

Oasis has been used for years by florists as a water-impregnated base for their floral arrangements, and in a few nurseries for ornamentals. Oasis foam is a fairly conventional, artificial, plastic foam substance, not unlike the material used to provide protection against knocking for some electronic appliances. Organically, it is neutral. It plays no role in the germination or sustenance of the seed, other than to provide the necessary support for the seedling, once it begins to emerge. The roots push through the foam and the sheet of oasis is then separated into individual cells, each with its plant, and placed in the hydroponic troughs to grow until harvest. The foam left on the root system is virtually unnoticeable. Oasis foam has the added advantage of being totally hygienic. There is no risk of introducing any disease into the system from the seed raising oasis media.

   The same product is also available in pre-stamped sheets, which are broken apart into individual cells ready for transplanting. The oasis foam sheets can be hand-seeded, or used in combination with automated seeder machines. Seeders are pneumatically operated, and a bank of needles sucks up one seed each, then drops them into pre-punched holes in each oasis cube. The size of the needles can be changed according to the size of the seed. There are less expensive versions of automatic seeders, which are more manual and require a little bit of 'muscle work', but are capable of filling a row of seeds once a second. There are 13 holes in a

A selection of lettuce seed raising media, plastic pots and cell trays

Lettuce seedlings 15 days after sowing into 'Oasis' cubes.

row of typical oasis sheet. The bonus of seeder machines is that they are 100% accurate.

Oasis sheets or cubes must be saturated with water prior to seeding, either by constant misting for one hour, or by hand drenching. Seeds are dropped into pre-punched holes - one per cube - and do not require covering with media. The oasis cubes must be kept moist during germination. To do this, either misting cycles or flood and drain type systems can be used. It is also possible to place the oasis sheets into a solid plastic tray, which remains constantly flooded with a shallow depth of water - at least one third the height of the cube. Once seeds begin to germinate, a dilute, complete nutrient solution should be applied at a conductivity level of CF 5 - 6 (0.5 - 0.6 mS/cm).

Rockwool or Growool

Rockwool is widely used to grow a range of crops from seedlings through to maturity. Rockwool is mostly made of diabase and limestone. These raw materials are heated to an extremely high temperature, at which point they become liquid. The liquid material is poured into a fast running disk in a spinning chamber, to form fibres. The fibres are supplied with wetting agent, pressed to a certain density and stabilised with a special binder into slabs. The slabs have a stable structure, are very porous and have a high water absorption capability - 80% water holding capacity and 17% air holding capacity.

Small rockwool propagation blocks are supplied in sheets, which can be separated to give each seedling its own root block when planting out. Rockwool does not break down during the life of the lettuce crop and is still present on the root system at harvest. Rockwool, however, is sterile and has an excellent water holding capacity. Rockwool propagation cubes can be seeded and treated in much the same way as oasis, however, rockwool has a higher water holding capacity than oasis and care should be taken to avoid over saturation of the media. As with oasis blocks, it is a good idea to thoroughly soak the rockwool propagation blocks in water (or even dilute nutrient solution as this adjusts the pH of the medium), prior to use. Rockwool is non-toxic, but can cause irritation due to the tiny spikes of material which can penetrate the skin, though this does not occur when the medium is wetted.

Compressed Peat Blocks/Pellets

Often sold as 'Jiffy 7's', these are peat pellets compressed into discs, contained by a nylon mesh. The discs are about 4cm in diameter and 1cm thick when dry. After soaking in water for 5 - 10 minutes, they swell to about 4 - 5 cm in height. Seeds are placed in the top, and left to germinate in the saturated media. As the seedling develops, the roots grow out through the nylon mesh. The entire block can then be placed into the hydroponic system. The use of compressed peat blocks for seedling production has largely been superseded by the use of oasis and other inert media, which is available at a lower cost and has been developed for use in automatic seeder machines.

MEDIA AND TYPES OF SEEDLING PROPAGATION TRAYS

While the use of individual media blocks has become more popular for lettuce seedling production, removing the need for plastic seedling trays and media, the cost of these products is greater than media-based systems. There is a range of inert medium which can be used to produce high quality lettuce seedlings. The most popular of these is either composted bark or vermiculite, placed in cell trays (200 cells per tray) or small plastic thin-walled pots. This method allows both precision automatic seeding or manual seeding, with each plant having its own separate rooting area.

Lettuce seedlings raised in cell trays and composted bark media

Oak Leaf lettuce seedlings, raised in plastic grow pots, ready for planting into an NFT system

The development of many inexpensive types of thin-wall individual pots has seen this method growing in popularity. Many larger operations now leave these pots on the root system at harvest, to avoid the added labour cost of removing them for reuse. Rigid cell trays can be reused, but require the extra step of extracting the seedling from each individual cell, without causing excessive root damage. Both thin-walled pots and cell trays can be filled with a range of inert media to support the germinating seed and developing seedling. The use of broadcast seed in open seedling trays is less popular, as it requires either later pricking out of the seedlings, or careful separation of the plants for placing into the hydroponic system. This method does not allow each seedling to have its own root block and excessive root damage can occur.

Composted Bark

The use of composted bark has become popular in the nursery industry as a peat substitute, and also provides an excellent seed germination media. Ground bark is composted, with lime additions to adjust the pH, and can later be sterilised. Using bark media in small cell trays often requires sieving, to remove larger particles and provide an even germination surface. Composted bark used for lettuce seedling production should not have fertiliser additions, so a dilute nutrient solution can be applied to the seedlings.

Small particles of bark can cause problems in an NFT system, so it is vital that a filter be attached to the return pipe to catch any bark particles which may find their way back to the tank, before blockages occur.

Perlite

Perlite is a silicaceous material of volcanic origin, mined from lava flows. The crude ore is crushed and screened, then heated in furnaces to about 750°C, at which temperature the small amount of moisture in the particles changes to steam, expanding the particles to small, sponge-like kernels which are very light. The high processing temperature gives a sterile product which is ideal for raising seedlings. Perlite will hold 3 to 4 times its own weight in water. It is essentially neutral, with a pH of 6 to 8, but with no buffering capacity. Unlike vermiculite, it has no cation exchange capacity and contains no mineral nutrients.

While this media does not decay, the particle size does become smaller by fracturing as it is handled. The finer grades are used as a seed germination media, but perlite can be mixed with other media, such as pumice or bark, to provide a more cost effective mixture. Care should be taken when handling fresh dry perlite, as its fine dust has a high silica content which, if inhaled, is both irritating and potentially damaging to the lungs. To settle the dust, the perlite should be sprayed with water inside the bag before handling.

Vermiculite

Vermiculite is a micaceous mineral containing water molecules between adjacent layers, which is expanded when heated in furnaces at temperatures near 1000°C. The water turns to steam, popping the layers apart, forming small, porous, sponge-like kernels. Heating to this temperature gives complete sterilisation. Chemically, it is a hydrated magnesium-aluminum-iron-silicate. When expanded, it is very light in weight, neutral in reaction, with a good buffering capacity. It has a high water absorption capacity and a relatively high cation exchange capacity, thus it can hold nutrients in reserve and later release them. Horticultural vermiculite comes in a number of grades, with finer particle sizes used for seedling production. Expanded vermiculite should not be pressed or compacted when wet, as this will destroy its desirable porous structure.

Pumice

Pumice is a silicaceous material of volcanic origin, that is essentially inert. It is a soft, light coloured, glassy rock with an appearance of a sponge, usually formed by the trapping of bubbles of volcanic gases in molten rhyolite. This type of rock is rich in silica, but poor in iron and magnesium. Pumice is highly porous, yet readily available moisture ranges from 22-30%

Seedlings - 5 days after sowing into perlite filled cell trays

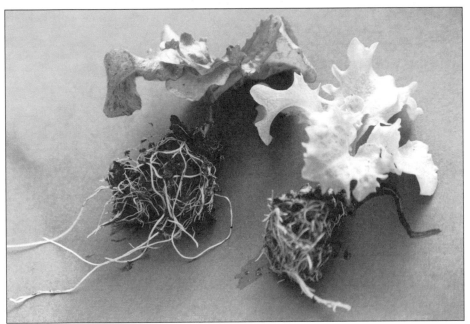

Seedlings after removal from cell trays (composted bark media), about to be transplanted into an NFT system.

of volume. Owing to the highly vascular nature of pumice, sufficient moisture is retained for the plant root to exploit, while the free-draining properties confer the advantage of good aeration. Finer grades of pumice can be used as a seedling media, however pumice is more often used in conjunction with a media which has a greater water holding capacity, such as perlite or vermiculite. Gritty particles of pumice may find their way into the final harvested product, so care must be taken when using this media. Pumice has the advantage as being available in a sterilised form at a reasonable cost.

Sand

Sand consists of small rock grains produced as the result of weathering of various rocks. Its mineral composition varies, depending upon the type of rock it was weathered from. It is generally best used in combination with other media, for a higher water holding capacity and lighter nature. Sand should be purchased in a pre-washed state, to eliminate any salt and silt which many contain fungi and weed seeds.

Scoria

Scoria is a porous volcanic rock. The hard red granules absorb water at a rate of 22% of their weight, by capillary action. Small particle size scoria (<6mm) is used in the Australian nursery industry in much the same way sand is used in media mixtures. Scoria is lighter than sand and more like pumice in nature.

Expanded Clay

Expanded clay has a physical structure much like pumice or scoria and is produced by baking specially prepared clay in ovens at 1200°C. The clay expands and the final product is porous and allows good entry of both water and air. The cost of expanded clay has not seen its extensive use in commercial hydroponics.

These are the most commonly used types of media for hydroponic lettuce seed raising. Other media types are also used on a limited scale, as selection is often dependent on the local availability and cost of the material.

GERMINATION AND SEEDLING DEVELOPMENT

The Germination Process

A lettuce seed consists of an embryo and its stored food supply, surrounded by protective seed coverings (seed coat). At the time the seed separates from the parent plant, the moisture content is low, metabolism is at a low level and no apparent growth activity occurs. The initiation of germination requires that three conditions must be fulfilled: first, the seed must be viable - that is the embryo must be alive and capable of germination; secondly, the seed must be non-dormant; and thirdly the seed must be given the right environmental conditions - water, correct temperate, supply of oxygen and, in the case of lettuce, light.

The first visible process that occurs during germination is the imbibition of water. Water is absorbed by the dry seed and the moisture content increases rapidly at first, then levels off. Initial absorption involves the imbibition of water by colloids of the dry seed, which softens the seed covering and causes hydration of the protoplasm. The seed swells and the seed coat splits. Water imbibition is a physical process and even dead seeds may swell, it is not an indication of the viability of the seed *(Hartmann and Kester, 1983)*.

After imbibition, enzyme activity begins, which activates the growth of the radicle (root). The first real visible evidence of germination is the emergence of the root, which results from the elongation of cells. The food reserves inside the seed are then mobilised and translocated to the growing embryo, to fuel the germination process. In the final stage of germination, the seedling plant results from the continued cell division in the separate growing points - the radicle and the emerging seedling leaves. While the reserves contained in the seed will fuel seedling development for a few days, the application of minerals is required for rapid seedling development and should commence as soon as the first two seedling leaves are fully expanded.

Seed Sowing - Water, Oxygen and Light

After initial wetting of the seed-raising media, no further watering should be required until after germination has occurred. This ensures adequate oxygen is retained in the media for germination to take place. Overhead watering of germinating seeds has been known to retard germination and is best avoided. An over-plentiful water supply often prevents germination, because oxygen is relatively insoluble in water. Too much water may also sometimes be damaging for poor quality seed, because the dehydrated cells cannot cope with such a rapid influx of moisture.

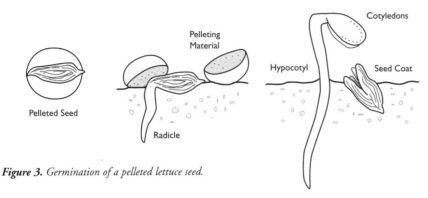

Figure 3. Germination of a pelleted lettuce seed.

An ideal seed bed should be well, but not excessively watered, and of a good structure so that there is plenty of aeration - hence the importance of selecting a good germination media. The early stages of germination, before the seedling has time to establish its own photosynthetic system (and thus produce food for itself), is one of the most vulnerable stages in a plant's life, especially if growth is slowed due to the onset of anaerobic conditions, when microbial attack can destroy a stand of emerging seedlings. Rapid germination is closely linked to successful plant establishment.

Lettuce seeds require light to germinate and for this reason are best left uncovered. Light is provided for pelleted lettuce seed when the pelleting material splits open after absorbing moisture.

Seedling Nutrition

At the time of full expansion of the first two seedling leaves, the plants should receive a complete dilute hydroponic solution, at a conductivity level of CF 5 - 6 (EC 0.5 - 0.6 mS/cm). The same formulation used to grow mature plants can be used, so long as it is in a dilute state. Research has proven that lettuce seedlings will develop faster at these lower solution conductivity levels, than if given normal strength solution. However, some growers do produce seedlings at a higher conductivity level (up to CF 20, or 2 mS/cm)), as this does produce harder, smaller seedlings which are better able to adapt to outdoor systems once transplanted. The solution conductivity can be raised from CF 5 to CF 10 (EC 0.5 - 1 mS/cm) at the later stages of development - in the 5- 7 days before being transferred into the hydroponic system. This helps the root system adjust to the higher conductivity levels the crop will be grown at, and hardens the plant for any transplant shock which may occur.

Planting out

Great care should be taken when separating the individual cell blocks, or seedlings, for transplanting into the hydroponic system. Any root damage will cause a possible entry site for disease pathogens and will result in a check to plant establishment and growth. Oasis and rockwool blocks must be separated very carefully, as the roots from each seedling will have grown into its neighbour's block and will need to be teased apart. Root damage can occur when seedlings are being extracted from cell trays also. The use of individual thin or thick walled PVC pots results in the least root damage to seedlings - each plant, with pot attached, is planted into the NFT gullies and this allows rapid root extension to occur.

DISEASE CONTROL DURING GERMINATION AND SEEDLING DEVELOPMENT

The most damaging and destructive pathogens are those resulting in 'damping off', which can cause serious loss of seeds, seedlings and young plants. In addition, there are a number of fungus, virus and bacterial diseases that are either seed-borne, or present in the water supply.

Damping Off Diseases

'Damping off' is a term long used to describe the death of small seedlings, resulting from attacks by certain fungi, primarily *Pythium ultimum* and *Rhizoctonia solani,* although other fungi - for example, *Botrytis cinerea* and *Phytophthora spp.* - may also be involved. Pythium and Phytophthora produce spores that are moved about in water. Damping off occurs at various stages during seed germination and subsequent seedling growth *(Hartmann and Kester, 1983).*

1. The seed may decay or the seedling rot before emergence from the media (pre-emergence damping off). This results in a partial or even total lack of seedling appearance.

2. The seedling may develop a stem rot near the surface of the medium and fall over (post-emergence damping off).

3. The seedling may remain alive and standing but the stem will become girdled and the plant stunted, eventually dying (wire-stem).

4. Rootlets of larger plants may be attacked; the plants will become stunted and eventually die (root rot).

The environmental conditions prevailing during the germination period will affect the growth rate of both the attacking fungi and the seedling. The optimum temperature for the growth of *Pythium* and *Rhizoctonia* is between 20° and 30°C, with a decrease in activity at both higher and lower temperatures. The moisture content of the germination medium is of great importance in determining the incidence of damping-off. Conditions usually associated with damping-off include over-watering, poor drainage, lack of ventilation, high density planting, or damage to the stem or root during transplanting. Young seedlings should always be handled by the leaves, never the stem.

Symptoms resembling damping-off are also produced by certain unfavourable environmental conditions in the seed-raising media. Drying, high media temperatures, or high concentrations of salts in the upper layers of the germination medium can cause injuries to the tender stems of the seedlings near the media surface. The collapsed stem tissue has the appearance of being 'burned off'. These symptoms may be confused with those caused by pathogens. Damping-off fungi can grow in concentrations of soil solutes which are high enough to inhibit the growth of seedlings. Where nutrient salts accumulate in the germination medium, damping-off can thus be particularly serious *(Hartmann and Kester, 1983)*.

Treatment for Damping Off Diseases

The control of damping off involves two separate procedures:

1. The complete elimination of the pathogens during propagation, by use of sterile media and fungicide sprays.

2. The control of plant growth and environmental conditions, which will minimise the effects of damping off, or give temporary control until the seedlings have passed their initial vulnerable stages of growth.

If damping off begins after seed germination, during seedling growth, it may be controlled by treating that area of the media with a fungicide such as Captan, Propamocarb (Previcur), or Metalaxyl (Ridomil). These should be sprayed over the seedlings, so long as the recommended rate is observed. Thiram is a protectant which may be used to prevent an outbreak of damping off. Another fungicide, Aliette (fosetyl-aluminium), also provides good control of damping off organisms and can be sprayed over the seedlings. Aliette is rapidly absorbed by the plants and translocated upwards and downwards in the sap stream. Aliette has the advantage of not only acting as a fungicide, but also stimulating the natural defence mechanism of the plant through the production of phytoalexin, making it less susceptible to attack.

Germination Problems

Failure to germinate can be a result of a number of causes, the most common being non-viable seed or excessive temperatures. Pelleted seed is particularly prone to failing to germinate if it has been stored for a period of time in an open packet and has absorbed water. Pelleted seed is rapid to germinate if sown directly after opening of the sealed packets. Raw seed can lose viability quickly if stored in warm, moist conditions. Seed subjected to temperatures in the mid to high 20s (Celsius) can enter a phase of secondary dormancy - which means it will no longer freely germinate until this dormancy has been broken (a period of refrigerated storage should solve this dormancy problem).

The most common cause of patchy germination or complete germination failure, is incorrect temperature. Seedlings are usually raised under cover in greenhouse conditions, which can cause temperatures to rise above the optimum for lettuce seed germination to occur. Once air and media temperatures approach 23°C, germination of raw seed will begin to be inhibited. Greenhouse temperatures can be cooled by the use of shadecloth covers, or misting of the atmosphere. Another cause of lettuce seed germination problems may be the damping off pathogens mentioned above, or uneven moisture content of the media (this is more common in cell tray systems).

CROP PRODUCTION PROBLEMS

Leaf coloration

Deep red pigmentation is desirable in the red varieties of hydroponic lettuce and this is promoted by several factors. Firstly, the colour potential of a lettuce leaf is genetic. Many varieties have now been bred, and are consistently being bred, which produce a deep red coloration in most conditions. A good example of this is the 'Lollo Rossa' cultivars now available to growers. The original 'Lollo Rossa' was a light green with pink tinged edges, whereas varieties such as 'Impuls' have now been bred which are an intense red colour all over the leaf surface.

Apart from the genetic influence on leaf colour, the pigments responsible for lettuce colouration are chlorophyll (green) and the anthocyanins (red). It is the mixture of these two pigments in the leaf that determines the colour - whether it be a brownish colour due to the presence of both, deep red due to the predominance of anthocyanins, or green due to the predominance of chlorophyll.

Both chlorophyll and anthocyanin concentration is dependent on the growing environment. Plants grown in shaded conditions will have a darker green appearance and less red pigmentation then those grown in full light. Anthocyanins are enhanced by high light levels and cooler conditions - thus resulting in the deepest red coloration during late winter and early spring. During the warmer conditions of summer, where rapid growth is taking place, the anthocyanin pigment becomes 'diluted' and this results in a less intensive red colour. Higher nutrient solution conductivity will promote more pigment formation and a deeper red colouration.

In order to obtain the deepest coloured lettuce, the best option is cultivar selection, since this is easier than providing the correct environmental conditions for maximum pigment development. Many cultivars are listed in commercial seed catalogues as having intensive red coloration during warmer season cropping. Growing the crop at the correct conductivity level will also ensure the colour potential of these cultivars is reached. Low conductivity of the nutrient solution will quickly result in dilute leaf colouration and should be avoided.

Some growers, through observation, can detect a drop in leaf colour immediately and correct this within 24 hours by increasing the level of potassium in the solution.

Temperature

Lettuce is a cool season crop and will produce the best quality plants in the cooler conditions of winter and spring. Lettuce will grow with night temperatures down to 4°C, but growth will be slower at temperatures below 8°C. If strict scheduling is required to meet market demands, or to allow successive crops to be planted on schedule, then heating to 8°C at night is recommended in greenhouse situations. Day temperatures are not critical and ventilation in both greenhouses and outdoor cloche systems should be given to provide day temperatures in the range of 12 - 21°C. Carbon Dioxide (CO_2) enrichment will speed up growth rates and improve head weight, but is of doubtful economic value for lettuce crops.

Lettuce plant spacing and densities

The density of plants per square metre is largely dependent on both the cultivar grown, as these differ markedly in size and shape, and the type of production system. Tiered or layered systems with gullies stacked above each other, require a greater plant spacing on the lower layers, so that sufficient light is intercepted by the plants in a greenhouse situation. Greater densities can be achieved on outdoor, bench type systems where there is only a single layer of plants and therefore maximum light interception. Larger varieties such as the 'Oak Leaf' and 'Salad Bowl' varieties require almost twice as much space as the smaller rounded red and green frill, or 'Lollo Rossa' types. It is therefore advisable to have separate parts of the hydroponic system (i.e separate benches) for the different sized cultivars.

In a greenhouse situation, it is usual to have the green varieties on the lower tiers and the red varieties on the top tiers, since these benefit the most from the higher light intensities which helps to intensify red coloration. As a guide, between 8 -24 plants per square metre of cropping area have been suggested for hydroponic production. Attention to correct plant spacing is important, as overcrowding of lettuce close to harvest increases the possibility of diseases such as Botrytis, which are extremely difficult to control when a dense leaf canopy prevents spray penetration. Over crowding also reduces the quality of lettuce heads, by causing 'stretching', with thin pale leaves, and results in a loose, floppy product.

CHAPTER ③ - CULTIVARS

CHAPTER ③ - CULTIVARS

INTRODUCTION

Potential growth in the fast expanding prepared lettuce market is predicted to be phenomenal. As lifestyles change, the demand for ready-to-use processed salads continues to rise. As a result, the breeding companies are looking for varieties with an intensity of colour and better taste and texture, as well as the production priorities of mildew resistance, and resistance to tipburn.

The hydroponic lettuce market is split into three groups:

• Whole heads for bagging

• Pre-packed chopped lettuce/salad packs

• Pre-packed baby leaves from young plants

Key factors for selection of lettuce varieties for pre-packing also include heads with an open frame and leaves that fall apart easily, with resilience of the leaf to the washing process. The consumer demand is more for the stronger colours - reds or greens rather than intermediate browns.

LETTUCE PHYSIOLOGY

Lettuce crops are harvested at the end of the vegetative growth phase and before entering a phase of reproductive growth (flowering). The objective with lettuce is to promote fast, bulky vegetative growth and this is particularly reflected in nutritional requirements.

Heading lettuce, such as the Butter Head varieties, form a considerable number of leaves (30+) before initiating a flowering stem, and in flowering the stem extends rapidly and terminates in a large number of flowers. The grower's aim is to quickly form as many leaves as possible, but to market the lettuce before there is any elongation of the flower stem. The rate of hearting in Butter Head and Crisp Head varieties is partly controlled by day length, and various Butter Head cultivars have been produced for hearting at different day lengths. The 'Triumph' Crisp Head variety will not heart in short winter days, and hence hydroponic crops of this variety are ready for market in early spring. It is important to select Butter Head varieties which will heart at the required time of year, and different varieties are available for all seasons.

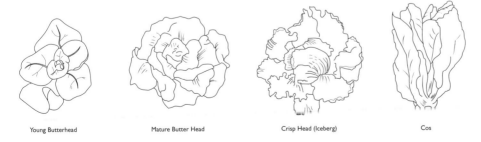

| Young Butterhead | Mature Butter Head | Crisp Head (Iceberg) | Cos |

***Figure 4.** Some Lettuce Types*

LETTUCE TYPES - THE MAIN GROUPS

The many different varieties of lettuce are often grouped into three types. The most common is head lettuce (often termed cabbage lettuce), of which there are the Crisp Head (or Iceberg) and Butter Head cultivars *(Figure 4)*. The Romaine, or Cos, type forms a loose, upright head. The 'leaf' lettuce types are non-heading and loose-leaved. The production of the leaf and Romaine types has increased dramatically in recent years, because of the increased popularity of tossed green salads.

The heavy, crisp Iceberg lettuce are more popular in America, and were developed to survive transport from California to the markets in the East. Loose, softer cabbage lettuce are more popular in northern Europe. Cos lettuce are widely grown in the Eastern Mediterranean. There are currently over 800 different kinds of lettuce grown in the US alone, with new varieties being constantly developed. In the USA the Iceberg or Crisp Head lettuce accounts for 74% of all production - the leaf lettuce 17%, and Romaine 9%. In Japan, the acreage of hydroponi-cally grown leaf vegetables such as lettuce, leaf onion and Honewort accounts for about 40% of the total hydroponic production area.

The gourmet or 'fancy' lettuce typically grown in hydroponics can be further grouped into several categories. The highly frilled types, also termed 'Coral' or 'Lollo Rossa', are mostly used for decorative reasons on platters and in salads. The Butter Heads, both red and green, are grown for their buttery texture and pleasant eating flavour for salads. The Salad Bowl types have finely divided leaves and are closely related to the red and green Oak types, whose leaves resemble an elongated oak leaf in shape. Then there are the Cos types with upright barrel shaped leaves, some with small spines, which are used in certain recipes (both hot and cold) and for caesar salads. Finally, there are the Loose-Leaved types, of which there are numerous variations of leaf shape, colour and size, none of which form a heart.

Crisp Head (Iceberg) Types

The Crisp Head types of lettuce have dense, firm hearted heads and crisp leaves and are the most important market garden soil-grown type. Crisp Head lettuce are grown in hydroponics, but are not as popular for hydroponic production as the fancy gourmet varieties. Strains of 'Great Lakes' and 'Imperial' mature about 75 days from planting. Other varieties include 'Triumph', 'Aspiring', 'Black Velvet' and 'Webbs Wonderful'. There is a selection of varieties for each season, some able to withstand frosts up to 1 degree (eg. Black Velvet), while others have bolt resistance (eg. Great Lakes) for summer production.

Smaller varieties of Crisp Head have become available for hydroponic or greenhouse production. Crisp Head lettuce generally do not receive the same prices as the more fancy varieties, due to the competition with market garden produced crops, which are available year round.

Butter Head (or Boston) Types

Greenhouse grown Butter Head lettuce is a high quality winter salad green, which has been extensively grown in England, Holland and other European countries for decades. Practically every leaf of this lettuce is edible when it is grown under protected cultivation. The heart is not as tight as that of a Crisp Head lettuce and the leaves are readily separated and broken up by hand to make up a salad. The inner leaves have an oily or buttery feel, which is where the name 'Butter Head' originates.

A bench of green and red Oak leaf lettuce nearing harvest.

In a well managed crop, every Butter Head lettuce planted will grow to a marketable size of around 240 grams. There are a wide range of both red and green Butter Head types, most of which are selected and bred for production at a particular time of year and for disease resistance. Butter Head lettuce develops best at night temperatures of around 7°C and day temperatures not exceeding 20°C. It will take 6 - 8 weeks from planting to grow a saleable product. In the early stages of the crop, the temperatures can be kept higher to induce faster leaf growth. When the first leaves are fully developed, the temperatures should be lowered again to improve heading. When Butter Head lettuce are grown under higher temperatures, the whole of their development tends to be loose, open and light in weight for their size.

Red loose leaf lettuce (cultivar 'Red Sails'), showing intense red leaf colouration during early spring

Butter Head (or Boston) Cultivars

There is a huge range of Butter Head cultivars available to commercial growers, with new varieties being introduced constantly. These cultivars are often grouped into size (small, medium or large frame) and season (winter or summer production). Some cultivars have disease (eg. mildew) and virus resistance. Seed catalogues often state the number of days to maturity and indicate whether the variety is suited to outdoor or protected cultivation. The standard variety is called 'Butter Crunch', from which many of the more modern cultivars have been bred. Some of the more commonly grown green butter head varieties include 'Esmeralda', 'Atlanta', 'Blondy', 'Big Boston', 'Conny' and 'Dolly'. Red Butter Head varieties are also available - some of these include 'Bibb' ('Merville des Quatre Saisons'), 'Caddo', 'Red Mignonette' and 'Manto'. There is a huge selection of others, which may be trialled in different cropping situations and systems before choosing the best variety. Cultivar selection is often an individual grower's choice.

Oak Leaf and Salad Bowl Types

'Oak Leaved' varieties were first listed by Vilmorin in 1771 under the name *'Laitue epinard'*. There are three main groups: Pale Green, Brown, and Dark Green. Oak Leaf is a loose leaf variety, with thin tender light green or brown/red leaves shaped like oak leaves, which form a rosette. Salad Bowl types are a development of the Oak Leaf types, which bolt less readily and have a more divided leaf shape. 'Royal Oak Leaf' is a modern selection, with darker green leaves and greater bolt resistance than the older green oak leaf forms. Both 'Red Oak Leaf' and 'Red Salad Bowl' form intensive brown/red pigmentation under cool conditions with high light intensity.

Butter Head variety 'Connie' nearing harvest in an outdoor system.

Oak Leaf and Salad Bowl Cultivars

Cultivars are often listed in seed catalogues as simply 'Red/Green Oak Leaf or Salad Bowl'. However, there are some newer selections available with more intensive red coloration and bolting resistance, including 'Stella' and 'Rebosa', which are Red Salad Bowl types. 'Pluto', 'Sherpa' and 'Carthago' are Green Oak Leaf types for year round production. 'Royal Oak Leaf' is a large, bolt-resistant, dark green oak leaf, suitable for summer production. 'Samantha' is a good Red Oak Leaf variety, with a compact habit and deep coloration which is ideal for hydroponic production. Oak Leaf and Salad Bowl varieties are often confused in seed catalogues, or sometimes just all referred to as 'Salad Bowl' types. 'Tango' is another Salad Bowl type, with deeply cut leaves which resemble an endive, however 'Tango' has little bolt resistance in warm weather and is a cool season variety only.

Lollo Rossa and Lollo Bionda (Red/Green Frill or Coral) Types

Lollo Rossa (red) and Lollo Bionda (green) are perhaps the most popular and widely grown hydroponic lettuce, along with green Butter Head varieties. The leaves are highly frilled at the edges and range from green tinged with pink, to a deep intensive red coloration for the Lollo Rossa cultivars. Lollo Bionda has the same highly frilled leaf type in a lime-green colour.

These varieties are used mostly as garnish, due to their highly decorative nature. Both Lollo Rossa and Lollo Bionda are loose leaf types and do not form a compact head, but do produce dense, rounded heads. The original Lollo Rossa type has a less intensive colouration than some of the newly developed cultivars and has little resistance to bolting in warm weather. There are now some highly coloured, larger framed Lollo Rossa varieties available for each season.

Left: Greenhouse grown 'Butter Head' lettuce crops at mixed maturity levels
Right: A tiered NFT system producing Lolla Rossa (top) and Lollo Bionda (Bottom) type lettuce under cover

Red Oakleaf in the foreground, Cos varieties in the middle, with Lollo Bionda types visible in the background.

Lollo Rossa and Lollo Bionda Cultivars

Selection of a good Lollo Rossa cultivar is important, if maximum coloration and good size is to be obtained. There are a number of Lollo Rossa cultivars available and newer improved varieties are being introduced to the market all the time. Lollo Rossa varieties include 'Atsina', 'Lollo Rossa Foxy', 'Impuls' and 'Pretoria'. 'Impuls' is a good standard variety of intensive red coloration and a medium frame size, with 'Pretoria' being an improvement on 'Impuls', with the added benefit of a larger frame size and higher bolting tolerance. Lollo Bionda (green) varieties include 'Casablanca' and 'Vanessa', which are similar to the original Lollo Bionda type, but have the advantage of a larger frame size, greater uniformity and resistance to bolting.

Loose Leaf (or Leaf Lettuce) Types

There are a great number of 'Leaf Lettuce' types which are placed in this category, simply because they do not produce hearted heads, or fall into the oak leaf or frilled categories. Both red and green Leaf Lettuce come in a variety of leaf sizes, shapes and a range of colour intensities. Leaf Lettuce are quick growing (approx. 45 days to maturity), with bolt resistant cultivars becoming increasingly available.

Loose Leaf (or Leaf Lettuce) Cultivars

Some of the more common green Leaf Lettuce varieties include 'Black Seeded Simpson', and 'Simpson Elite' - these are very early, loose leaf types which produce ruffled, slightly frilled light green, crisp leaves. 'Simpson Elite' has more bolt resistance than 'Black Seeded Simpson' and a more ruffled leaf shape. 'Green Ice' is another green leaf or loose-head variety, which has crisp-textured glossy green leaves which are crinkled or savoyed with wavy and fringed leaf margins. 'Green Ice' is slow to bolt and can form very large, heavy heads under good growing conditions.

There are also a large number of red Leaf Lettuce in a range of colours from light green-brown to intensive red/crimson colouration. One of the oldest and most popular of the red types is 'Red Sails' - a batavian loose leaf with crinkled, deep bronze red leaves. 'Red Sails' is slow to bolt and is a very popular variety in North America, both for hydroponic and outdoor soil production. There are a number of improved 'Red Sails' varieties - 'Red Fire' is one which produces greater uniformity of size and a deeper red colour, with ribs which are less subject to breakage. All 'Red Sails' types have excellent bolt resistance and can be grown year round. Other red loose 'Leaf' types include 'Rosalita' and 'Rossimo', 'Batavia Red', 'Royal Red', 'Red Regency', 'Goya', 'Red Head' and many others, all with differing degrees of red coloration, leaf shape, size and head weight.

Cos (or Romaine) Types

The Cos varieties are the oldest type of lettuce grown. Wall paintings in some Egyptian tombs are thought to represent a narrowly pointed form of Cos lettuce, which are thought to have been cultivated around 4500 BC. The Cos or Romaine type of lettuce develops an elongated head of stiff upright leaves, about 80 days from planting. It is an important lettuce in Europe and is gaining popularity in other countries.

Cos lettuce are used in dishes, both hot and cold, and are designed to be eaten rather than used as a garnish, like the more decorative lettuce types. Both red and green Cos varieties are available. White Cos is a variety which forms a tight head inside, which the inner leaves blanch white.

Red Salad Bowl grown in an outdoor bench system.

Winter grown, outdoor Lollo Rossa (left), Crisphead (centre), and Lollo Bionda (right).

Mature outdoor NFT grown Crisp Head (Iceberg) lettuce type.

Cos (or Romaine) Cultivars

Green Cos varieties include 'Cos-Verdi' - a tall, barrel-shaped lettuce with dark green wrapper leaves; 'Toledo' - a shorter 'Cos' type and early maturer; 'Diamond Gem' and 'Little Gem', which are small Cos varieties. Other green Cos types include, 'Cosmic', 'Lobjoits Green', 'Marvel' and 'Romance'.

There are also a number of 'semi-Cos' types, which are half way between a Cos lettuce and a Butter Head. These include 'Winter Density', 'Pavane' and the 'Little Gem' types. Other varieties are the 'Paris White Cos', which forms the white blanched inner leaves and 'Red Cos' (syn. 'Rouge d'Hiver', 'Red Winter', 'Red Romaine') which are Cos or Romaine lettuce with red leaves, tolerant of both heat and cold.

OTHER HYDROPONIC SALAD GREENS

Endive and Chicory

These two vegetables are closely related to one another, both being in the genus *Cichorium* from the family Asteraceae (which also contains the Lactuca, or lettuce, genus). Endive differs from chicory, mainly in being annual rather than perennial. The leaves of chicory are often hairy, those of endive always hairless. Both have a long tradition as salad plants, especially in the Mediterranean region where many different forms are cultivated. Chicory and endive are essential salad ingredients in Europe, where endive, escarole and chicory are just as important as lettuce. An Italian or French cook would not serve a salad without at least one of these greens.

In French, the names of chicory and endive are reversed - endive is the name for the forced shoots of *Cichorium intybus*, while *chicor'ee fris'ee* is the cut-leaved form of *C.endiva,* and Scarole the name for broad-leaved Batavian endive.

Sugar loaf chicories and endive are grown in a similar way to lettuce, but are slower to mature than lettuce and may have bitter leaves which require blanching during production.

Chicory and Endive Cultivars

Chicory - Italian and Catalogna Types *(Cichorium intybus)*

The most commonly grown Italian chicory produced hydroponically is 'Raddichio' or 'Corn Lettuce'. Raddichio has a sharp, tangy flavour and red/white colour. These chicories are uniquely Italian and are grown for summer and winter season salads and cooked dishes. The decorative colourful leaves are used as an attractive garnish or added to salads. Varieties include 'Guilio' - a red Radicchio for spring planting; 'Castelfranco' - a striped-speckled chicory with variegated red and yellow foliage; and 'Red Verona' chicory - with deep red leaves and a solid heart.

'Catalogna' chicory is also termed 'Asparagus Chicory', 'Italian Dandelion' or 'Radichetta'. These types of chicory have deeply cut, broad dandelion-like leaves, rapid growth rates and can be used as salad or cooking greens all year round. Varieties include 'Puntarella', 'Del Veneto' and 'Giant Chioggia'.

'Chicory - Grumolo' is another type of chicory, which is rather bitter and is used to blend in with salad mixes. Varieties include 'Grumolo Verde Scukro', 'Grumolo Biondo', 'Spadona', 'Trieste Sugar' and 'Suckerhut'.

Endive *(Cichorium endiva)*

Endive salad greens produce tender succulent leaves, which are bitter when green, but can be used to replace lettuce in salads throughout the year. Varieties include 'Tres Fine Maraichere' (Frisee), which has extra finely cut lacy leaves and bolt resistance, 'Reffec Green Curled', 'White Curled', 'Italian Fine Curled', and 'Saint Laurent', all differing in the degree of leaf curl and green colour.

Hydroponic Herbs

A huge range of herbs is now being produced in hydroponics, both for sale of the individual plants (with roots attached) in much the same way lettuce is sold, and as fresh-cut products for the restaurant and catering trade. Small herbs are well suited to hydroponic production, requiring much the same environmental and nutritional conditions as lettuce. With the increasing awareness and use of the more unusual salad greens such as Chicory, Cress and Rocket, fresh herbs are increasing in demand. Some of the more widely grown herbs in hydroponic production are Basil (of which there is a large range of types), Chervil, Chives, Dill, Fennel, Mint, Marjoram, Oregano, Parsley, Rocket, and Thyme.

Mesclun Mixes (Mesclun or Saldist)

This is a mixture of salad greens which are sown thickly and eaten young, the leaves being cut and the plants encouraged to re-sprout. These mixtures may contain all or most of the following: Lettuce, Endive, Chicory, Dandelion, Chervil, Rocket, Mustard and even Buck's Horn Plantain. The origin of this type of salad mix is in the south east of France. Harvest is approximately 4 weeks after sowing, when the seedling mix is 7-10 cm high.

GROWER VARIETY TRIALS

Commercial growers often carry out their own assessment of new varieties, to determine their potential performance in their system. This is recommended for all commercial growers, as certain varieties will perform better in one system on one site than they may do on another. Trial packets of seed can be obtained from most commercial seed suppliers for evaluation by growers.

Trials of new varieties should be carried out through two or more seasons, to determine the cultivar's suitability for summer and winter cropping. Particular attention should be paid to a cultivar's resistance to problems such as tipburn and bolting, as well as the colour potential of red varieties. As part of the selection and evaluation process for new cultivars or different varieties, a grower should also assess the shelf life qualities of the lettuce. Plants should be grown to maturity, harvested in the normal way, and kept for a number of days in both refrigerated and room temperature storage, to determine how long each will store. This will also highlight any post-harvest quality problems which may arise - such as tip browning, susceptibility to bruising, wilting and post harvest rots.

CHAPTER ④ - HYDROPONIC SYSTEMS

CHAPTER ④ - HYDROPONIC SYSTEMS

INTRODUCTION TO HYDROPONIC SYSTEMS

Entry costs into the hydroponic industry are greater than traditional market gardening, but installation expense need not be high. Although most hydroponic systems are housed in greenhouse structures, primarily to achieve maximum environmental control and year round cropping, hydroponic growing does not demand a greenhouse.

Plastics have also reduced the cost of many components used in hydroponic systems. As the industry grows and the volume of materials used increases, the overall cost per unit will come down further. Hydroponic gullies for example, manufactured in white UV-stabilised PVC, in lengths up to 9 metres long, have a guaranteed life of 10 years or more with maintenance being virtually zero, and prices have fallen in the last 10 years as volume has increased.

NFT - Nutrient Film Technique

The nutrient film technique (NFT) was developed during the late 1960's by Dr Allan Cooper, at the Glasshouse Crops Research Institute in the U.K. With the NFT system, a thin film of nutrient solution flows through plastic channels, which contain the plant roots with no solid planting media. The root mat develops partly in the shallow stream of recirculating solution and partly above it. It is extremely important to maintain this basic principle of a nutrient 'film', because it ensures the root system has access to adequate oxygen levels. The key requirements in achieving a nutrient film situation are described by Cooper (1996) as being:

1. To ensure that the gradient down which the water flows is uniform and not subject to localised depressions, not even a depression of a few millimetres.

2. The inlet flow rate must not be so rapid that a considerable depth of water flows down the gradient

3. The width of the channels in which the roots are confined must be adequate to avoid any damming up of the nutrient by the root mat, since if inadequate, it is to be expected that yields will be directly proportional to channel width.

4. The base of the channel must be flat and not curved, because there will be a considerable depth of liquid along the centre of a channel with a curved base, merely because of the shape of the base *(Cooper 1996)*.

A principal advantage of this system in comparison with others, is that a greatly reduced volume of nutrient solution is required, which may be more easily heated during the winter months to obtain optimal temperatures for growth, or cooled during hot summers to avoid bolting and other undesirable plant responses.

Lettuce in NFT

Lettuce have been grown in NFT for many years. Some of the earliest systems used ordinary wide span greenhouses with concrete floors, in which narrow gullies were cast for the NFT solution. Other early installations used selected profiles of long-run roofing steel, with baked epoxy finishes. Over recent years, systems have become more intensive. Some of these systems attempt to make better use of greenhouse space, by using various vertically-spaced gully systems or

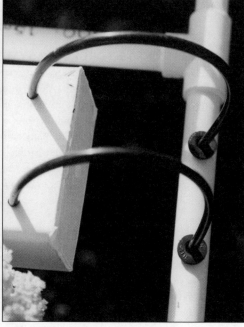

Left: NFT-grown lettuce removed from gully, showing planter pot and root system development
Right: Nutrient solution delivery system into NFT gully.

horizontal systems, with movable gullies to permit spacing to be adjusted as the lettuce grow. Rectangular PVC gullies are usual for these systems. One experiment compared gullies between 60 and 150mm wide and found that 80mm wide gullies, 40mm deep with a slope of 1.5%, were best. A flow rate of 0.2 litres/minute was optimum when these gullies were 3.1 metres long.

The slope of the channels in an NFT unit need not be severe. A drop of 1 in 50 to 1 in 75 appears suitable, although 1 in 100 is not sufficient. Depressions in the channel floors must be avoided, because ponding of immobile solution will lead to oxygen depletion and growth retardation. Some NFT system designs are constructed with adjustable stands so optimum slope can be obtained for each stage of crop growth. Although this is effective in eliminating ponding, this design increases capital costs. In long-run installations, it is possible to introduce the nutrient solution at two or three different points along their length to ensure good aeration.

Types of NFT Systems and Gullies

There is a huge range of NFT system designs, with most incorporating the use of some type of PVC gully supported by benches, in both outdoor and greenhouse situations. Many growers take advantage of both square and round diameter downpipe and incorporate these into systems of their own design. Most large commercial growers purchase PVC gullies in bulk and can reduce costs in this way. The most commonly used type of PVC gully is the rectangular, white 150 x100mm channel *(Figure 5)*. Over recent years, a number of other, smaller types of channels have been developed, designed specifically for lettuce and other small crops such as herbs and strawberries. Channels such as these usually have pre-punched holes for planting seedlings into, and removable lids which aid in cleaning of the system. The choice of gully system or material is often based on availability, cost and grower preference.

With lettuce being a small plant, NFT gullies are often tiered or stacked in greenhouses to make maximum use of growing space *(Figure 6)*. Shelf-like systems can be stacked up to 8 layers high, although this does reduce the quantity of light reaching the lower layers. Most systems use a 3-layer stack, in order to achieve maximum growth rates without yield losses due to low light on the lower layers. While this stacking of the gullies is most beneficial where space is limited, such as in a greenhouse, outdoor systems sometimes use this method also. The majority of outdoor systems and a number of greenhouse operations grow the crop on a one layer bench at waist height. Rigid gullies are usually 6 - 8 across the bench, which allows easy access for planting and harvesting operations. These outdoor bench systems are also often constructed to allow some sort of crop cover, such as a simple cloche frame, as the crop needs protection from wind, heavy rain and hail.

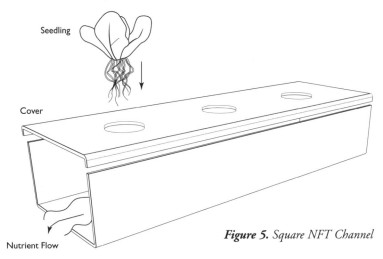

Figure 5. *Square NFT Channel*

Rigid multi-channel sheeting has found a use in hydroponics, for smaller sized crops such as lettuce. These require greater support from the bench structure, but have the advantage of providing a number of small channels per sheet, and are easier to clean. Other systems use channels constructed of timber and lined with plastic film, such as panda film. Layflats or gusset channels have been used in the past for greenhouse lettuce production. This is a flat tube of polythene, which is unrolled onto a prepared smooth surface.

NFT and Rockwool
In this system, plants are established on small rockwool slabs, which are then positioned in channels containing recycling nutrient solution. This system has the advantage of the rockwool block acting as a reservoir of nutrient solution in case of pump failure, and also helps to anchor the plants in the NFT channel.

Short-Run Hydroponics
Regardless of what shape or size the NFT channel may be, the length of the 'run' is of great importance. There has been a tendency to construct very 'long runs' of gully to reduce the number of emitters required in a system. Excessively long channels can cause a number of

Figure 6. *Tiered NFT System*

problems, including temperature rise or fall of the nutrient solution over the length of the channel, reduction in nutrient and oxygen levels and a reduction in growth from one end of the channel to the other. Channel length can vary from 3 metres to well over 20 metres in some systems. The use of short-run channels (less than 3m), is not widespread but is an alternative type of system to the traditional long-run type of hydroponics.

The theory behind the use of short-run channels is that even a small plant such as a lettuce, has a huge root surface area capable of absorption of oxygen and nutrients. Therefore, solution entering the top of a gully and flowing past even a small number of plants, actually passes over several square metres of root surface. Nutrient flowing down a short-run channel (less then 3 metres in length) will only pass a limited number of plant root systems before it is returned to the tank, remixed, oxygenated, temperature adjusted and returned back into the system. Therefore, no differences in nutrient, pH, temperature or oxygen loss will exist along the length of a channel, as they might with very long-run gullies.

Recently, the building industry has seen the development of a number of brands of inexpensive short-run roofing material. While the corrugations of these rigid sheets conduct water extremely well, the length of the sheets is designed for ease of handling and installation.

Top: Greenhouse lettuce crop grown in tiers - 6 layers high
Bottom: Outdoor crop grown under cover, - 2 tiers high

While it may not be practical to lap these sheets to create a long series of channels in hydroponics, as the joint would have to be sealed to prevent plant roots growing between the lapped sheets, this material has proved ideal for the development of short-run systems. The productive life of these materials, due to their rigid, non toxic, UV protection properties, is just as long as for other types of gullies.

Top: 'Short-Run' system benches under construction, using corrugated roofing material as NFT channels.
Bottom: Short Run system with a crop of Butter Head lettuce being harvested.

Other NFT Systems

Most of the early greenhouse lettuce crops were produced on the greenhouse floor, in channels of cast concrete painted with epoxy resin. In a typical installation for year-round lettuce production, the concrete was formed into parallel channels 10cm wide, 2.5cm deep and 45m long, on a slope of 1 in 50. While this type of installation was common in the

1960's and 70's, the use of less expensive plastics in the hydroponic industry has lead to this system becoming less common.

Movable channels

Although the capital cost of movable channel systems is higher than fixed bench systems, this method allows maximum use of greenhouse space, as the plants are moved apart as they grow and expand. This type of system was first used in the US and Canada, but has been adopted by growers around the world. This variable plant spacing technique is designed to maximise space utilisation and leaf interception of light.

Movable benches covered with corrugated sheets have been used as lettuce planting troughs in some systems. Plants are set in the corrugations, through which nutrient flows, at close intervals when young, and spread out as more growing space is needed. Benches are movable to allow access to growing areas.

Mechanisation

Some movable bench systems have been designed to allow automated harvest of the NFT grown lettuce. The 25cm wide troughs are covered with a flexible plastic material, through which the lettuce are planted through holes. At harvest, a winching machine pulls the covering material, lettuce and all, up an incline to be rolled up on a spool. As the plastic moves upslope towards the winch, a mechanism removes the lettuce head, which then moves off on a conveyor belt toward the packing station.

Pipe Systems

A-frame type systems have been developed for high density lettuce production. Seedlings are planted in sloping plastic tubes (slope of 1 in 30) and arranged in horizontal tiers, resembling A-frames in end-view. This system, developed for use with Dutch Venlo glasshouses, effectively doubles the usable growing surface and accommodates a plant density of 40 per square metre. A vertical pipe system has also been developed, much like those used to grow strawberry plants. Small diameter plastic pipes, 1.3m long, are suspended by overhead wires above a nutrient solution-collection channel. Germinated lettuce plants are squeezed into holes (20-28 per pipe) in the sides of the tubes, and nutrient solution is pumped into the top of each pipe, to drip down through the tubing and plant roots. Vertical NFT systems using plastic piping are relatively costly, and have not been widely adopted in commercial operations.

FLOATING HYDROPONICS

These types of systems usually consist of a large tank or shallow pond of nutrient, upon which the developing plants float, supported by lightweight materials such as polystyrene *(Figure 7)*. In 1980, researchers at the University of Arizona designed and developed a prototype hydroponic CEA raceway lettuce production system. An 0.5ha greenhouse containing 0.26 ha of water surface in 10 production raceways, as well as nursery, packaging and research areas, was operated year-round. The design's production rate was 4.5 million heads/ha/year. While the design of the tanks is where the name 'raceway' came from, the nutrient solution is stagnant and does not flow. The raceways used in the prototype system were each 4m x 70m and 30cm deep. The nutrient solution was monitored, replenished and aerated.

This type of floating hydroponics has two distinct advantages. The nutrient 'pool' is a virtually frictionless conveyor belt, for planting and harvesting from the movable floats, and the plants are spread in a horizontal plane so that interception of sunlight by each plant is maximised.

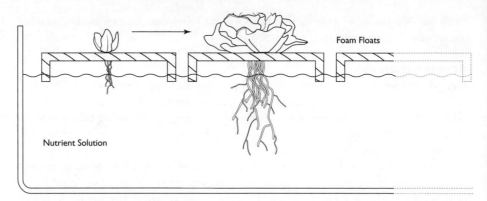

Figure 7. *Floating Hydroponic System*

Two to three week old seedlings are transplanted into holes in the 2.5cm thick plastic floats, in staggered rows with approximately 300 cm^2/plant. Time to harvest is reported as being 4 - 6 weeks, depending on season. As a crop of several floats is harvested from one end of a raceway, new floats with transplants are introduced at the other end. Long lines of floats with growing lettuce can be moved easily at the touch of a finger *(Jensen and Collins, 1985)*.

AEROPONICS - ROOT MIST TECHNIQUE

In a different application of closed-system hydroponics, plants are grown in holes in panels of expanded polystyrene or other material, with the plant roots suspended in mid-air beneath the panel and enclosed in a spraying box. The box is sealed so that the roots are in darkness, to inhibit algal growth and to produce saturation humidity. A misting system sprays the nutrient solution over the roots periodically - for a few seconds every 2 - 3 minutes. This is sufficient to keep the roots moist and the nutrient solution aerated.

An advantage of this technique is that twice as many plants may be accommodated per unit of floor area as in other systems, due to the A-frame design of the chambers, and hence the cubic volume of a greenhouse is better utilized *(Figure 8)*.

AGGREGATE HYDROPONIC SYSTEMS

In aggregate hydroponic systems, a solid inert medium provides support for the plants. As in liquid systems, the nutrient solution is delivered directly to the plant roots. Also, aggregate systems may be either open or closed, depending on whether surplus amounts of the solution are recovered and reused. Open systems do not recycle the nutrient solution, whereas closed systems do.

Open Aggregate Systems

In most hydroponic systems, excess nutrient solution is recovered. However, in an open system the surplus is not recycled to the plants, but drains to waste underneath the growing troughs or bags. Because the nutrient solution is not recycled, such an open, drain-to-waste system is less sensitive to the composition of the medium used, or to the salinity of the water. These systems are also associated with less capital cost of set-up and the use of inexpensive, often reusable media. Irrigation is usually programmed through a timer and in larger installations, solenoid valves are used to allow only one section of a greenhouse to be irrigated at a time.

As open systems are less sensitive than closed systems to the type of growing media used, a great deal of regional ingenuity has been displayed in locating low-cost inert materials for

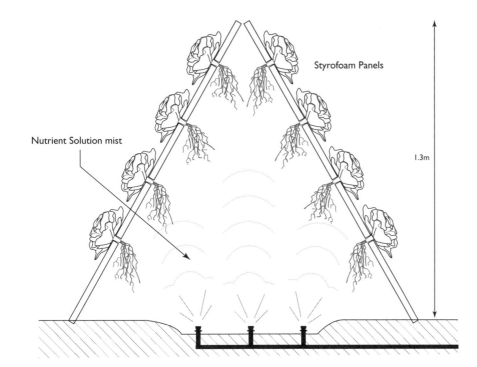

Nutrient Solution mist

Styrofoam Panels

1.3m

Figure 8. *A-Frame Aeroponic System*

drain-to-waste systems. While pumice is popular in New Zealand, due to its easy sourcing and inexpensive nature, overseas growers rely on materials such as sand, gravel, vermiculite, sawdust, peat, bark, perlite and mixtures of two or more of these medias.

Bag Culture

Bag culture systems are similar to drain-to-waste trough/bed culture, except that the growing medium is placed into plastic planter bags, which are formed in lines on the growing area, thus avoiding the costs of forming beds or troughs. The bags may also be used for at least two years and come in a range of different sizes. The evaporation rates from such media systems can be very high in summer, thus concentrating the nutrient solution in the media. As a result, drain-to-waste media systems are often given a lower strength solution than would be used in an NFT installation. This type of system is more commonly used for crops such as tomatoes and cucumbers, but has been used successfully for lettuce.

Closed Systems - Flood and Drain

Closed systems using gravel as an aggregate material were commonly employed for commercial and semi-commercial hydroponic units in the 1970's. This technology has mostly been super-seded by NFT systems, or by newer open aggregate systems.

A typical sub-irrigated gravel closed system of the early type, consists of a growing bed filled with coarse sand/gravel, or any other similar inert non-phytotoxic medium, with a subgrade piping system, a supply tank or sump containing the nutrient solution and a pump to deliver the solution to the growing bed *(Figure 9)*. A timing mechanism was attached to the pump to allow regular flooding and draining of the beds. In these systems, the solution is flooded into the bed to within about 2cm of the surface of the medium and then drains by gravity back into the sump for reuse. Such systems are capital intensive because they require leak-proof growing beds, as well as subgrade mechanical systems and nutrient storage tanks. Water proofed concrete was initially used and later fibreglass, or heavy-gauge plastic film to form the growing beds.

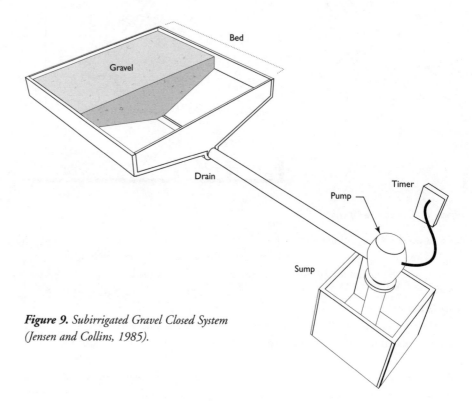

Figure 9. *Subirrigated Gravel Closed System (Jensen and Collins, 1985).*

NON-RECIRCULATING CAPILLARY SYSTEMS

Aeration or circulation of the nutrient solution is routinely recommended for hydroponic crops. However, low-maintenance systems have been developed which do not require power or complex equipment and are relatively low in cost.

Non-circulating hydroponic systems have been described, in which a small pot or some other plant container rests on or above a layer or screen. The screen encourages root development and provides an anchor for plant support. The lower part of the plant container must be submerged in nutrient solution immediately after transplanting. As the plants grow, the nutrient solution level must be lowered gradually to a point just below the screen. The correct

Top: Construction of gravel media beds for hydroponic lettuce production.
Bottom: Gravel media beds after planting.

management of the nutrient solution level is very important for the proper establishment of transplants. Kratky (1993), described a method of capillary non-circulating hydroponics for the production of leaf and semi-head lettuce, which was developed at the University of Hawaii.

Outdoor lettuce crops being grown in planter bags containing gravel media. Each bag and plant receive nutrient solution via an emitter from a gravity-fed, manually operated supply tank.

This system consisted of a shallow plastic lined tank with a painted timber lid placed over the tank. Nutrient solution with a pH of 6.5 and EC of 1.0 mS/cm (CF 10) was placed in the tank to a depth of 75mm. Seedlings were produced in tapered plastic containers of media and were placed into the top of the tank cover at 18 days of age, so that 47mm of the seedling container extended above the surface and 158mm remained below the timber cover. The bottom 25mm of each container was immersed in nutrient solution and the resulting capillary action was sufficient to wet the medium throughout the containers, thus automatically watering the plants. No additional maintenance was required from this time until harvesting. The benefits of this system are that after the lettuce are transplanted into this system, no additional watering, fertilisation, or monitoring of pH or electrical conductivity was required. Thus, the only cultural operations required for this system are preparation of the nutrient solution, planting, harvesting, clean-up and pest and disease control.

It was found in this system, that plant growth was not affected adversely when the nutrient solution level drops or remains constant. However, severe wilting or even death can occur after a significant rise in the nutrient solution level. Once roots have become acclimatised to a microclimate of moist air, they can no longer tolerate submerged conditions. Therefore, this method is not suitable for outdoor production, as rainfall would cause the nutrient level to rise *(Kratky, 1993)*.

CHAPTER ⑤ - HYDROPONIC SYSTEM ENGINEERING

CHAPTER ⑤ - HYDROPONIC SYSTEM ENGINEERING

By Simon Lennard B.Hort.Sc

SETTING UP A SYSTEM

Prior to the construction of a commercial hydroponic system, several factors need to be calculated to ensure the system operates effectively, and sufficient nutrient solution is maintained in circulation. These factors include the size of nutrient tank, pump, delivery pipes, and drainage channel. Other factors to take into consideration are gully length and the slope of both the gullies and drainage channel.

GULLY SIZE AND SLOPE

The main objectives in determining the length, width and slope of gullies, are to ensure that they are large enough to hold the root system of the crop, no ponding occurs and that the solution flows at a constant rate down each gully. Gullies should be constructed of sufficiently rigid material, or be well enough supported that their slope and cross section remains constant along their entire length. To ensure adequate oxygenation of the root zone, a physiological limit is placed on the length of gullies - usually no more than 40m, and preferably less than 30m.

One litre of solution is enough to provide a 2mm deep film, 100mm wide and 5m long at zero slope. For a gully 20m long therefore, a 1 litre/minute flow of nutrient solution will take four minutes to produce the required depth across the entire surface of the gully. That is, a 20m long gully, 100mm wide with a solution depth of 2mm, will hold four litres of solution. Using this example, it is easy to calculate the solution volumes and flow rates required in a standard lettuce system. Other factors such as the cohesive properties of nutrient solutions to the gully base and sides, the tendency of solutions to flow in 'trickles' rather than complete films, and the effect of gully slope, curvature, and flow from the ends, complicate the calculation of solution flow and depths in an NFT gully. However, the following simple formulae can be used to obtain a good guide to system requirements:

Volume in gully at 0 slope (V) litres = 1000 x L x W x D (m)

Where: L is the length (metres),
          W is the width (metres),
          D is the depth (metres) of solution in the gully
          (if the gully has a round section, W x D should be replaced by $[(W/2)^2 \times 3.1416] \times D/W$

Nutrient "Turnaround" at 0 slope (minutes) = F/V

Where: F is flow rate in litres per minute,
          V is the volume of the gully in litres
          and solution Velocity (metres/minute) = flow (m^3/minute)/cross sectional area (m^2)

The slope of the gully will determine the effect of flow rate on depth, due to its influence on solution velocity. A higher slope will allow a greater volume of water to flow at a shallow depth, while conversely, reducing the slope of the gully will produce a greater depth of solution at a proportionally slower flow rate. Therefore, a steeply sloping gully will accommodate a higher flow rate while maintaining a shallow depth of film and so produce better oxygenation of the nutrient solution. A less steeply sloping gully will require a lower flow rate to achieve the same result of shallow depth and oxygenation, and this in turn reduces the length of the gully in terms of the number of plants the reduced flow (and hence lower volume of oxygenated solution) can support. If longer gullies are required, the slope and flow rate should be increased. The limits this places on physical access to the gullies at the top end, also limits gully length in NFT systems.

The delivery pipe and drainage channels should be selected to supply sufficient volume to and from each gully. The flow rate to be supplied by the delivery pipes can be calculated, by multiplying the flow rate into each gully by the number of gullies. The drainage channel can be treated as a gully, using the formulae below, when considering the size, slope and cross section required to carry each volume of solution back from each set of gullies to the nutrient tank.

Drainage channel cross sectional area (m^2)= 1.2* (V/1000 x n) / l

Where: V is the volume of solution in each gully (in litres)
          n is the number of gullies per drainage channel,
          l is the length of the drainage channel (in metres)

*the factor 1.2 allows a 20% over-estimate of channel size to prevent flooding.

TANK SIZE

Usually a "buffer" capacity of at least 50% is allowed for in the selection of a tank size for an NFT system. This means that when all the gullies are carrying nutrient solution at the desired depth, sufficient nutrient remains in the tank to half fill it, or the tank is large enough to hold twice the amount of nutrient held in the gullies. This is considered to be a minimum requirement and most systems will have significantly larger tanks than this. The term 'buffering capacity' is due to the effect of the increased volume in reducing the rate of change of the mineral content over time, as a larger volume of nutrient will require less frequent additions of stock solution to correct EC, than a smaller volume. The size of nutrient tank can easily be calculated using the following formula:

Minimum Tank Size (l) = 2000 x N x L x W x D + L_1 x (d_1 x .5)^2 x 3.1416
$$+ L_2 \text{ x } (d_2 \text{ x } .5)^2 \text{ x } 3.1416$$
$$+ L_3 \text{ x } (d_3 \text{ x } .5)^2 \text{ x } 3.1416....$$

Where: N is the number of gullies
          L is the length of the gullies (metres)
          W is the width of the gullies (metres)
          D is the depth of the solution in the gullies (metres)
          L_1 is the length of delivery pipe (metres)

Above: Concrete nutrient tank below floor level inside a greenhouse
Below: Nutrient tank for an outdoor NFT bench system

d_1 is the internal diameter of the delivery pipe (metres)
L_2, d_2, etc are the lengths and ID of any subsequent delivery pipes (metres)

This figure should be added to the volume of solution returning to the tank in the drainage channels : Lc x Wc x Dc (m), where Lc is the length, Wc is the width, and Dc is the depth of solution in the drainage channels.

If gullies of different configurations are used in the same system, then the calculation will have to be repeated for each set of gullies, and the results added to give the total volume.

These formulae assume square section gullies and drainage channels. For round sections, the components W and Wc should be replaced by $(d/2)^2$ x 3.1416, where d is the internal diameter of the round gully in metres.

PUMP SELECTION

Most hydroponic systems utilise centrifugal pumps, which are capable of producing a constant flow of nutrient solution, rather than the pulsating flow associated with piston or diaphragm pumps. Centrifugal pumps will either pump a small volume of water to a high head, or conversely a large volume of water to a low head. In between the two extremes, the characteristics of each pump will vary, depending on the power of the motor and the impeller type and impeller case design.

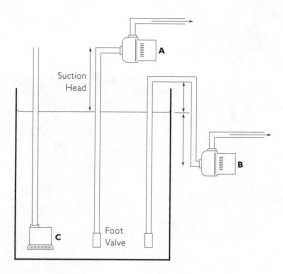

Figure 10. *Pump Performance Curves and Suction Heads*

Pump manufacturers will usually provide details of the pump flow vs head characteristics, usually in the form of performance curves. It is important to remember when selecting a pump, that the total head to which a pump will deliver nutrient solution, combines the suction head and delivery head. That is, as the pump begins to lower the level of nutrient in the tank, the delivery head will decrease, as the suction head is increased. Any centrifugal pump, no matter how powerful, has a maximum suction head of just over 10m, as atmospheric pressure prevents suction from greater depths. *Figure 10* shows the measurements of suction head - note that the operating suction head is measured from the surface of the solution, not from the end of the suction pipe.

The compromising effect of suction head on delivery head can, of course, be overcome by positioning the pump below the surface of the nutrient in the tank, either outside the tank (b), or by using a submersible pump (c).

As well as the physical height of the system, the delivery head also includes the frictional loss caused by pumping water through pipes and fittings. This frictional loss is termed 'head loss' and is stated in metres head loss per hundred metres of pipe, or metres per fitting. Tables of head loss are available from pipe manufacturers and sales outlets. In general, head loss becomes more per metre of pipe, as pipe internal diameter decreases, and as the angle of bends in fittings increases and their internal diameter becomes less. The pressure of solution leaving the emitters should be added to the head loss and total head of the system, to achieve the operating head required by the pump.

The volume of flow delivered by the pump is able to be calculated from multiplying the number of gullies, by the flow rate required in each gully. Having worked out the total operating head as above, it is then a simple matter of finding the right point on the pump's performance curve, ensuring sufficient volume is delivered at the right operating head, to select the most suitable pump for the system.

Due to the effect of head loss along a length of pipe, and the reducing flow as solution passes through emitters along the pipe, the pressure and flow along a lateral will decrease. The laterals must therefore be large enough to carry the required flow to all emitters. This again is calculated by multiplying the flow required from each emitter, by the number of emitters along a lateral, and ensuring the pipe's internal diameter is sufficient to carry this flow. Provided sufficient nutrient solution is in circulation, in order to equalise the flow from all emitters in the system, a ring-main arrangement is usually recommended, and this involves simply joining all the laterals together to form a 'ring'. There will still be some variation, particularly at the outer edges of the ring, but this will be minimised.

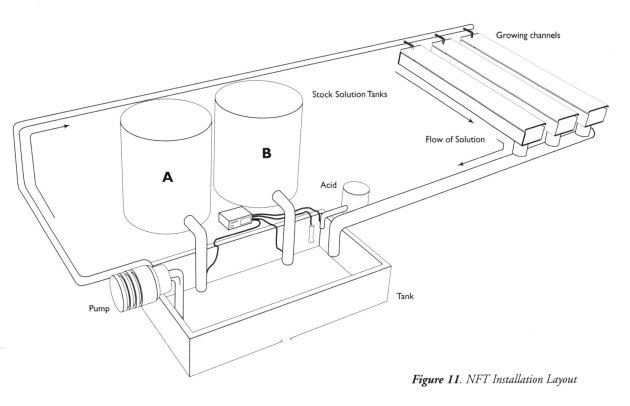

Figure 11. NFT Installation Layout

Increasing the pressure of water in a small diameter pipe, will not improve the flow of water as much as increasing the pipe size to the maximum allowed by the pump. Consequently, if the flow appears too low from some emitters, it is more effective to increase the diameter of the delivery pipes, rather than invest in a more powerful pump. As most hydroponic systems do not require water to be under much pressure at the emitter's end, it is usually better to select a pump capable of producing a large flow of water at just above the minimum required head. This will allow for extension of the system at a later stage, as the increase in flow required is likely to be proportionally more than the increase in operating head.

SYSTEM LAYOUT

All systems require a well designed layout, to allow ease of maintenance, cleaning and efficient delivery of the nutrient solution. A nutrient holding tank with associated stock solution, acid tanks and pumping equipment is usually housed either inside the greenhouse, or in an enclosed building in outdoor systems. From here the solution is pumped via a series of pipes and emitters to the growing beds or channels *(Figure 11)*.

CHAPTER ⑥ - SYSTEM MAINTENANCE

CHAPTER ⑥ - SYSTEM MAINTENANCE

ELECTRICAL CONDUCTIVITY (EC or CF)

Electrical conductivity (EC) is a measure of the dissolved nutrient salts in a hydroponic solution. As the nutrients are taken up by a plant, the EC level drops, since there are fewer salts in the solution. The EC of the solution can also be increased when the water is removed from the solution, through the processes of evaporation and crop transpiration. If the EC of the solution increases, growers lower this by adding pure water. If the EC decreases, it can be increased by adding quantities of concentrated nutrient stock solution.

ELECTRICAL CONDUCTIVITY (EC) MEASUREMENT

Water conducts electricity, usually because it is full of impurities such as small amounts of chemical salts. How well a solution of water and salts will conduct electricity can be measured by a simple device - an EC, CF or total dissolved salts (TDS) meter. These meters consist of two electrodes which are placed in the solution to be measured. When power is supplied, an electric current passes from one electrode through the water to the other electrode. The meter displays how much of the electric current is flowing between the electrodes and this is displayed as either EC, or CF, or in some cases parts per million (ppm).

There are several units of measurement used to express conductance in a hydroponic solution. The most universal unit is millisiemens/cm (mS/cm, or mS cm^{-1}), which may also be expressed as millimhos/cm (mho). One mMho/cm = 1 millisiemen/cm (mS cm^{-1}). Conductivity factor is also used in horticulture, and this is obtained by multiplying millisiemens by 10 to give a whole (not a decimal) figure to the range of conductivity levels at which horticultural crops are grown. While the range of EC levels used in hydroponics for various crops ranges between 0.5 and 8 mS cm^{-1} (CF 5 to 80), lettuce crops are usually grown at the lower end of the EC range, between 0.5 and 2.5 mS cm^{-1} (5 - 25 CF units).

Solution concentration can also be measured in parts per million (ppm). The total concentration of elements in a nutrient solution should be between 1000 and 1500 ppm, so that osmotic pressure will facilitate the absorption processes by the roots. This should correspond to a total salt conductivity level of between 1.5 and 3.5 mS cm^{-1} (15 and 35 CF).

While EC is a good measurement of the total amount of dissolved salts, it does not differentiate between which individual salts are in the solution. EC also varies not only with the concentration of salts present, but also with the chemical composition of the nutrient solution. Some fertilizer salts conduct electric currents better than others. For example, ammonium sulphate conducts nearly twice as much electricity as calcium nitrate, and more than three times that of magnesium sulphate, whereas urea does not conduct electricity at all. Nitrate ions do not produce as close a relationship with electrical conductivity as do potassium ions. The higher the nitrogen to potassium, the lower will be the electrical conductivity values for the nutrient solution. *Table 1* shows the relationship between different fertiliser salts and the conductivity produced in water.

Since conductivity readings change with solution temperature, it is important to either use a temperature compensating EC meter, or take all readings at a standard temperature (i.e 20°C / 68°F). There are temperature compensation factors for correcting conductivity data, but most modern meters for hydroponic use now have built in temperature compensation systems.

Table 1. Conductivity comparisons (EC) of 0.2% solution in distilled water (Resh, 1987).

Fertiliser compound	EC (mMho)	CF
$Ca(NO_3)_2$ Calcium nitrate	2.0	20
KNO_3 Potassium nitrate	2.5	25
NH_4NO_3 Ammonium nitrate	2.9	29
$(NH_4)_2SO_2$ Ammonium sulphate	3.4	34
K_2SO_4 Potassium sulphate	2.4	24
$MgSO_4.7H_2O$ Magnesium sulphate	1.2	12
$MnSO_4.4H_2O$ Manganese sulphate	1.55	15.5
KH_2PO_4 Mono potassium phosphate	1.3	13
HNO_3 Nitric acid	4.8	48
H_3PO_4 Phosphoric acid	1.8	18

SOLUTION pH LEVELS

The pH of a hydroponic solution is a measure of the number of hydrogen ions. The pH of a solution can range between 0 and 14. A neutral solution has a pH of 7. Solutions ranging from pH 0 - 6.9 are considered acidic and have a greater concentration of H+ ions. Solutions with pH 7.1 - 14 are basic or alkaline and have a greater concentration of OH- ions.

The pH of a hydroponic solution is important, because it controls the availability of nutrient salts. For hydroponic lettuce production, a pH range of 5.6 - 6.0 is acceptable. Nutrient deficiencies may occur at levels above or below the acceptable range, the reason being that certain elements or salts are only available to the plant within a certain pH range. A pH value should be selected which provides the best uptake conditions for the crop. This value is between pH 5.8 and 6.5 for most plants, however, plants can survive in the pH range 5 through to 7.5. Below pH 5 there is a danger of burning and destroying the root tissue of the plant. Above pH 7.5 some of the nutrients may precipitate out of solution and become unavailable to the crop.

THE EFFECT OF pH ON THE AVAILABILITY OF ESSENTIAL ELEMENTS

Iron, manganese and zinc become less available as the pH is raised from 6.5 to 7.5 or 8.0. Molybdenum and phosphorus availability is affected in the opposite way, being greater at the higher pH levels. At a very high pH level, the bicarbonate ion (HCO^{3-}) may be present in sufficient quantities to interfere with the normal uptake of other ions and thus is detrimental to crop growth.

pH ADJUSTMENT

Many municipal water supplies vary considerably in their initial pH, thus effecting the pH of the hydroponic solution. Rain water is close to neutral, while many bore water supplies can be either acid or alkaline, depending on the surrounding soil and mineral content of the water. pH can be easily corrected through the addition of either acid or alkaline solutions. An acid is a substance which, when added to the nutrient solution, will ionise to provide hydrogen ions. For example, nitric acid (HNO_3) ionises to H+ and NO^{3-}. A base (or alkaline) is a substance which ionises to provide hydroxyl ions. For example potassium hydroxide (KOH) ionises to K+ and OH-.

Acids are either termed strong or weak, depending on the degree of ionisation they undergo in solution. Strong acids such as hydrochloric acid, in a dilute solution will undergo 100% ionisation, whereas a weak acid like acetic acid will only undergo about 4% ionisation. The acids commonly used in hydroponics to lower the solution pH are phosphoric acid (H_3PO_4) and nitric acid (HNO_3). Potassium hydroxide (KOH) is used to increase pH. Most growers use phosphoric acid to lower pH, as this is less hazardous than the highly corrosive nitric acid. Phosphoric acid has the advantage of adding small amounts of phosphorus to the solution.

Acids for pH control are usually purchased in concentrated form. A 10% solution of either nitric or phosphoric acid is adequate to adjust pH levels. Nitric acid, however, in concentrated form is extremely corrosive and will cause burns if splashed onto the skin. A 10% solution should be prepared in advance, and stored for either manual or automatic pH adjustment. When the local water supply is very acid, it may be necessary to add an alkali such as potassium hydroxide (KOH) to raise the pH into the recommended range. Potassium hydroxide is usually purchased in a pelleted form and should be prepared into 5% solution (i.e 50 grams of pellets into 950mls of water). Potassium hydroxide, while not corrosive, will however, stain the skin yellow and should be handled with care.

pH TESTING

pH can be tested with either automatic meters, or with the use of pH paper test strips, or aquarium/swimming pool testing kits. A pH meter is a type of sensitive volt meter, which measures the pressure of electricity. Pure water has no voltage, but acid or alkaline solutions produce a small amount of electricity. This amount of electricity produced is too small to be measured by an ordinary volt meter, so pH meters have amplifiers which increase the output of the pH probe placed in the solution. The voltage signal produced in the probe, once it has been amplified, is then conditioned by special circuits to allow for temperature difference, because pH readings are affected by temperature in much the same way as EC readings. The meter then produces a digital readout, giving the pH value of the solution *(Dalton and Smith, 1984)*.

The major problem with pH meters, is that readings can become inaccurate if the meter is not regularly calibrated and the probe replaced every 12 months. Buffer solutions of pH 4 and 7 are used to check and recalibrate pH meters.

pH test strip papers are a less expensive alternative to electronic pH meters, however they are not as precise. A strip of paper is removed from the roll, dipped into the solution to be tested and the colour which forms on the strip is then compared to a chart provided. This gives an indication of the range of pH of the solution (for example from 6.2 - 6.5) and is adequate for use with domestic hydroponic units. Test kits, such as those used to measure the pH of aquarium or swimming pool water, are also available. These work in much the same way as the test strips. A tablet is added to a small volume of solution and the colour measured against a colour chart.

WATER SUPPLY

Good quality water is the number one basic requirement for any hydroponic system. It is important that a potential grower have a full water analysis carried out on the water supply, whether it be bore or town supply water. In many cases, microbiological tests may also be carried out to determine if any potential pathogens are present in the water supply. The water in a hydroponic system must have no toxic properties, or be easily treated to produce pure water. Even water supplies which are safe to drink by the World Health Organisation's drinking water standards, may not be suitable for hydroponic production. Many drinking water supplies contain chlorine for example, which although tolerated by humans, can have devastating effects on hydroponic crops. Lettuce are particularly susceptible to chlorine damage, which results in root death and necrosis of the leaf. High levels of sodium can also result in poor lettuce growth, if levels exceed 35 ppm, and many treated town water supplies use caustic soda (sodium hydroxide) to raise pH, which reduces pipe corrosion, thus increasing sodium.

Town water supply authorities can normally supply intending growers with a water analysis, although the composition of the water can change at any given time, depending on how the original dam source is treated to bring it up to acceptable drinking standards. If the water is obtained from a bore, dam or stream, it is important this is analysed regularly as these sources too can change as ground water levels fluctuate over the season.

The most common problems encountered with water supplies which will effect the hydroponic solution, are common salt (Sodium Chloride, NaCl) and Iron (Fe), particularly where ground water is sourced from iron sand soils. Calcium (Ca) and Magnesium (Mg), often from areas with a high percentage of limestone soils, and less commonly Bicarbonate (HCO_3), and Boron (B) may also be present. Salt or sodium chloride is a common problem in water supplies of coastal regions. While chloride is a trace element, many affected water supplies have levels of this element in excess of what plants require. Some crops, such as tomatoes, can tolerate high levels of sodium chloride, whereas tender leaf crops such as lettuce cannot. Since sodium chloride tends to accumulate in solution, as it is not taken up to a great degree by plants, frequent dumping is recommended in areas (such as New Zealand) where salt exists in nearly all water supplies.

Iron (Fe^{2+}), is another micronutrient, but in this form it will oxidise and precipitate out as a rust coloured powder - this makes it unavailable as an iron source to plants. Bores from iron sand country often have a system of aerating the water, followed by settling or filtration to remove the iron sludge, since this will block drippers and pipe lines.

Calcium (Ca) and magnesium (Mg) are present in what is termed 'hard water'. They are, however, useable as major nutrients in hydroponic solutions, but the chemical composition of the nutrient formula will need to be adjusted to allow for this.

Bicarbonate (HCO_3) is also found in hard water. It is not a usable nutrient, but will act to raise the pH of the hydroponic solution and needs to be neutralised with acid (either phosphoric or nitric). Boron (B) is another micronutrient which may be present in some water supplies, but this is usually present at such low levels, that it does not cause a problem. However, Boron should be left out of the nutrient formulation to prevent any toxicities from occurring.

WATER STERILISATION

The most common methods of water sterilisation are chlorination and UV light, however other methods such as micro filtration and ozone treatment are becoming more popular. Water treatment costs vary with the impurities found in the water and the volume to be treated. A simple ozone water treatment plant, with a 5000 litre storage tank, treatment pump and ozone injector, will be expensive but will provide a sterile water supply of up to 50, 000 litres a day. Ozone treatment can also be used for the removal of iron (Fe) and manganese (Mn) from base water.

The commercial use of ozone for water sterilisation, primarily by municipal water suppliers, has been around for nearly a century - the gas is manufactured by a generator, which electrically charges air which passes through a chamber. This corona discharge method changes the oxygen (O_2) content in the chamber into ozone (O_3). The resultant gas is unstable and attempts to react with other elements nearby, in order to release the extra oxygen atom. The ozone is injected into the water via a venturi system attached to a centrifugal pump, and contaminants are then oxidised by the gas. Once the process is completed, the oxygen which remains in the water can be taken up by the plant. Ozone treatment produces highly oxygenated water which is ideal for hydroponic use. Cost of daily treatment is low and no chemicals are added to the water. Ozone (O_3) reverts back to oxygen (O_2) in a few minutes after injection into the water, making it a very safe and natural way to treat water. Ozone is one of the strongest and most rapid sterilising agents, many times stronger than chlorine and UV light.

Reverse osmosis can also be used to remove unwanted minerals from water supplies intended for hydroponic use. Reverse osmosis is extremely efficient at removing most dissolved salts to very low levels. The membrane required in the reverse osmosis process is, however, expensive and the life of the membrane is dependent on the water quality being pumped through it. Often, iron (Fe) and other suspended matter should be settled out before treatment. Reverse osmosis has been used in arid areas to make sea water drinkable and usable for hydroponics, but is an expensive method of obtaining pure water in most situations.

NUTRIENT STERILISATION

One of the problems with recirculating hydroponic systems is the possibility of contamination by microbial plant pathogens. If contamination occurs, it can be spread rapidly throughout the entire system by the circulating nutrient solution, and thus has the potential to produce serious economic loss. Several methods of removing bacteria and fungi from water are available, including the use of ultraviolet sterilizer lamps, inline filters (0.22m), ozone treatment and chlorination.

The results of a study evaluating the effects of nutrient sterilisation by UV, suggest that removal of bacteria from the nutrient solution slightly inhibits growth between 7 and 14 days, and slightly enhances it between 14 and 28 days. This indicates that bacteria affect the uptake of nutrient elements by plants. In general it appears that rhizoplane bacteria enhance nutrient uptake in young seedlings, but inhibit both nutrient uptake and translocation in older plants *(Schwartzkopf et al, 1987)*. UV sterilisation also causes problems with iron in solution. UV can cause iron to precipitate from solution a few hours after sterilisation has taken place. This can occur to the point where no measurable concentration of iron is present in the solution after 24 hours.

Chlorination is sometimes used by growers to help control pathogens in the nutrient solution. Chlorine is only effective on exposed pathogens, such as those suspended in water or those on the surface of plant roots, the growing system or media. Chlorine does not kill pathogens it cannot contact, such as those which have already infected and invaded root cells, causing disease. Because chlorine can damage plant roots, lower rates of chlorine are added to recirculating nutrient solutions than to water treated for town supply. 1ppm chlorine is recommended for recirculating nutrient solutions, as concentrations greater than this may be toxic to the crop.

THE GREENHOUSE ENVIRONMENT

While a greenhouse provides excellent protection from climatic factors such as wind, rain and hail, which often lower the quality of the product, and also serves to increase the rate of growth, it is essential that the environment be controlled to provide the correct conditions for lettuce crop growth. The most important of these is temperature. Lettuce is a cool climate crop, so attention to correct temperature control - particularly during the summer months - is essential. Lettuce crops require less light than crops such as tomatoes and cucumbers, however the use of tiered systems which maximise greenhouse space, means that maximum light penetration is also of importance. Having reflective white plastic flooring material will assist with reflecting light back onto the plants on the lower tiers, as will painting all greenhouse structures white.

Selection of a cladding material will also influence light penetration into the greenhouse. Both glass and PVC films transmit satisfactory amounts of solar radiation, however, while glass is opaque to reradiation, polythene is not. This is a disadvantage of this material and at night, under clear sky conditions, it is possible that an unheated polythene structure may have temperatures lower than that outside. This is because energy is being lost by radiation, it is not being released back by clouds and there is no opportunity for warm air to move in to replace the cold air inside. In practice, this problem is often overcome by the condensation of water on the inside of the film, since water is opaque to reradiation *(Fisher, 1989)*.

NUTRIENT HEATING AND COOLING

NFT allows an efficient way of heating the plant roots, which may also raise the temperature of the surrounding air. The biological effects (and energy savings) of heating and cooling plant roots rather than manipulating the temperature of the much larger air volume, is evident in many crops. Winter grown lettuce benefits from root heating when the plants are small and close to the heated solution. However, experimental trials at the University of Arizona, reported that there was no increase in growth due to increased solution temperature, when 2.5 cm thick expanded plastic sheeting was present between the plants and the solution, apparently because of the insulative effect of the plastic.

In warmer climates, NFT permits an economical cooling of plant roots, avoiding the more expensive cooling of the entire greenhouse. Problems occur in hydroponics when the temperature of the nutrient solution exceeds 20°C (68°F), as this causes 'bolting' in lettuce crops. Channel surfaces in NFT systems may be coloured white to maintain lower nutrient temperatures. Cooling the liquid for lettuce production not only reduces bolting, but lessens the incidence of the damping off fungus Pythium, which causes plant damage and death, particularly of smaller seedlings.

AIR TEMPERATURES

Temperature is a major controller of the rate of plant growth. Generally, as temperatures increase, chemical processes proceed at faster rates. Most chemical processes in plants are regulated by enzymes, which perform at their best within narrow temperature ranges. Above and below these temperature ranges, chemical processes begin to slow down or stop completely.

Left: Outdoor lettuce benches showing shade cloth (32% shade) covers which help reduce air temperatures over the summer months
Right: A and B stock solution tanks feeding into the nutrient tank. Potassium solution tank can also be seen for additional K supplementation

At this point, the crop becomes stressed, growth is reduced and the plant may eventually die. The temperature of the plant environment should be kept within optimum levels for fast and successful maturation. The lettuce is a cool season crop, performing best at temperatures lower than other salad crops, such as tomatoes and cucumbers. However, there is a selection of cultivars which do well in most climates, from cool to very warm. Temperatures between 8° and 24°C result in the best growth, although lettuce crops can survive light frosting. At temperatures above 25°C (77°F), lack of seed germination and premature bolting of crops can become a problem.

Air temperatures can be reduced in both outdoor and greenhouse cropping situations by a number of methods. Solution cooling is particularly effective for reducing crop temperature stress in lettuce and is used in many tropical climates. Shading of the crop with covers is also effective at reducing air temperatures by up to 5 - 8 degrees under summer conditions. There is a range of materials available for use as thermal screens, for both greenhouses and cloche systems. These may consist of shadecloth materials or 'micro-clima' woven material. In general, the greater the thickness or weave of the material, the greater the shading effect and loss of light levels. In summer conditions with high light levels, it is possible to use a 32 - 50% shade-cloth cover without reducing radiation enough to effect plant growth and yields.

In a greenhouse situation, the main method of temperature control is ventilation. It is important that the sensors controlling the heating and ventilating systems are measuring the correct air temperature. Exposed thermostats can be heated up directly by the sun, responding therefore to a temperature which could be 10°C above the actual air temperature. Aspirated screens are used in greenhouse situations to rectify this problem. The screen is an insulated box containing a small fan, which is continually moving a sample of the greenhouse air through the box and over the sensing element of the thermostat *(Fisher, 1989)*. These screens are placed in the centre of the greenhouse, just above crop height. From the readings taken at the aspirated screen, ventilation or heating can be triggered to adjust the environment inside the cropping area.

There are two types of greenhouse ventilation commonly used by growers. These are 'natural' ventilation caused by the replacement of the warm air inside the greenhouse with the cooler air outside, and fan ventilation in which air is drawn in through a vent and across the greenhouse to an extractor fan. With 'natural' ventilation, the rate of cooling is dependent on the temperature gradient, the outside wind velocity and its direction in respect to the vents, and the amount of ventilator opening. In a greenhouse with an adequate amount of ventilation, 60 air changes per hour can occur when there is a significant gradient between inside and outside the house. An 'air change' is used to describe the replacement of all the air in the greenhouse with fresh air from outside. This is usually expressed as air changes per hour.

RELATIVE HUMIDITY LEVELS

The relative humidity (RH) of the air influences the transpirational water loss from plants. High RH, whether it be in a greenhouse or outdoors, causes less water to transpire from the plants, which causes less transport of nutrients from the roots to the leaves and less cooling of the leaf surface. High humidities can also cause disease problems such as Botrytis and mildew, which thrive in moist conditions. Low humidity levels can also cause problems such as inducing drying and burn of leaf margins.

ALGAE

Algae is a type of plant growth which looks like a green to black coloured stringy slime. Algae growth can become a problem in hydroponic systems where light is allowed to enter the system. Algae does not adversely effect the crop if present in small amounts, however it does tend to block emitters and filters. Algicides are available for hydroponic use, the products containing chelated copper (10 - 11%) as an active ingredient being the most effective and least likely to damage plants.

CROP TIMING

Lettuce crops can take about 10 - 12 weeks to mature in winter, and 6 - 7 weeks in summer. Lettuce growers report that NFT results in 30 - 50% faster growth than soil crops.

CO_2 ENRICHMENT FOR GREENHOUSE LETTUCE CROPS

While CO_2 enrichment is used extensively for greenhouse crops such as tomatoes, it is not often applied to lettuce crops, which mature more rapidly and at lower temperatures. The CO_2 concentration of the greenhouse air directly influences the amount of photosynthesis (growth and production of sugars) by the plants. Normal outdoor CO_2 levels are around 350ppm, and plants in a closed greenhouse during the day can deplete the CO_2 concentration to very low levels and thus severely reduce the rate of photosynthesis. In greenhouses, increasing CO_2 concentration to 600 - 1200 ppm speeds up growth, but must be added in a pure form to prevent any problems from impurities such as ethylene gas. As an alternative, since CO_2 enrichment is expensive and not often warranted in lettuce crops, good ventilation during the daylight hours will ensure adequate levels of CO_2 are present.

FILTERS

With any NFT system, it is essential that filters be present, preferably both inline and at the return into the tank. Media, pieces of root system, algae, insects and other contaminates all find their way into NFT systems and can cause blockages. Inline filters are useful for removing fine sediment and vegetative matter from solution before it reaches the emitters, while a coarser filter attached to the return pipe will catch other contaminates before they collect in the holding tank.

A number of materials are available for filters. A very effective method is to use aquarium filter wool, contained within a stocking, attached to the return gully outfall. This will not only remove coarse pieces of material, but will help remove any algae from the system.

AUTOMATIC DOSING SYSTEMS

Most large commercial growers use automatic dosing units, which regularly check the solution CF, and pH level and adjust these with controlled additions of nutrient stock solution, acid or water. Many different types of automatic controllers are available and these help take some of the manual labour out of hydroponic growing.

CHAPTER ⑦ - LETTUCE NUTRITION

CHAPTER ⑦ - LETTUCE NUTRITION

LETTUCE NUTRITION IN HYDROPONIC SYSTEMS

The roots of the lettuce crop absorb mineral nutrients as ions from the nutrient solution. One of the reasons why hydroponically grown lettuce plants produce such rapid growth, is that all the nutrients they require are always available to them in the right proportions, as well as a constant supply of water in which the nutrients are dissolved.

The process by which the mineral nutrients dissolved in the hydroponic solution are absorbed by the plant's root system, is called osmosis. Osmosis is the tendency of fluids to pass through a semi-permeable membrane, such as those contained on the root hairs. A semi-permeable membrane is one that will allow some substances to pass through, but not others. In plants, the root hairs allow nutrients dissolved in water to enter the root system, but exclude other particles such as crop debris or sediment, which may also be in the solution. This works by the cells in the plant root hairs containing a dense solution of salts and organic acids. Since this solution in the root cells is stronger than the weak solution of nutrients dissolved in the water, this results in a strong osmotic pressure driving the weak nutrient solution in through the cell walls, to dilute the dense solution in the root. This process of osmosis continues from cell to cell, so that the nutrients dissolved in the solution enter the plant's roots, eventually moving through the whole plant. There is also, within plant systems, active transport of some ions against a concentration gradient.

However, osmosis can also work in reverse. If the concentration of the hydroponic solution is too high, (higher than the concentration of cell contents in the root system), the plant will lose water to the nutrient solution and begin to wilt.

Once the nutrients have entered the plant through the process of osmosis, they pass into the plant's xylem tissue. This is a network of vessels which transport the nutrients around the plant for continued cell growth and development.

MAJOR ELEMENTS REQUIRED BY LETTUCE CROPS

There are 18 mineral elements necessary or beneficial for plant growth. Carbon (C), Hydrogen (H) and Oxygen(O_2) are supplied by the air and water. The six macronutrients, Nitrogen (N), Phosphorus (P), Potassium (K), Calcium (Ca), Magnesium (Mg) and Sulphur (S), are required by plants in large amounts. The other elements are required in small amounts and are termed trace elements or micro nutrients. The essential trace elements include Boron (B), Chlorine (Cl), Copper (Cu), Iron (Fe), Manganese (Mn), Sodium (Na), Zinc (Zn), Molybdenum (Mo) and -most recently reported - Nickel (Ni).

There are other elements termed 'beneficial elements' which are not essential for all plants, but are required by some species of plants. Beneficial elements include Silicon (Si) and Cobalt (Co). The distinction between 'beneficial' and 'essential' is often difficult in the case of some trace elements. Cobalt (Co), for instance, is essential for nitrogen fixation in legumes and may also inhibit ethylene formation in cut flowers, but has not been shown to be of great benefit to lettuce crops. Silicon (Si), which is deposited in cell walls, has been found to improve heat and drought tolerance and increase resistance to insects and fungal infections. Silicon, acting as a beneficial element, can help compensate for toxic levels of Manganese (Mn), Iron (Fe), Phosphorus (P) and Aluminum (Al), as well as Zinc (Zn) deficiency, and may be of benefit to lettuce crops.

TISSUE ANALYSIS

Table 1

Lettuce leaf tissue analysis commonly produces the following N, P and K concentrations (as a percentage of dry weight) in whole plants:

N	P	K	Ca	Mg	S
3.4-4.5	0.4-0.6	4.5-6.0	1-1.7	0.14-0.27	0.25-0.5

Trace elements (as ppm)

Fe	Mn	Zn	Cu	B	Mo
100-200	40-150	25-40	5-15	30-50	0.1-1 ppm

FUNCTIONS OF THE MACRO, MICRO AND BENEFICIAL ELEMENTS

This is a brief outline of the role of essential and beneficial mineral elements that are required for good lettuce crop growth.

Carbon (C)

Carbon is a constituent of all organic compounds found in plants.

Hydrogen (H)

Hydrogen is contained in all organic compounds of which carbon is a constituent. Hydrogen is important in cation exchange relations.

Oxygen (O_2)

Oxygen is a constituent of many organic compounds in plants. Only a few organic compounds, such as carotene, do not contain oxygen. Oxygen is also involved in anion exchange between roots and the external medium. It is a terminal acceptor of H+ in aerobic respiration.

Nitrogen (N)

Nitrogen is one of the main elements contributing to the growth of a plant. Plants use nitrogen to produce amino acids and proteins, which are used to produce new cell growth. Nitrogen is a major component of proteins, hormones, chlorophyll, nucleic acids, vitamins and enzymes essential for plant growth. Nitrogen moves easily throughout the plant, servicing new growth at the expense of the older foliage.

Phosphorus (P)

Phosphorus is necessary for seed germination, photosynthesis, protein formation and most aspects of growth and metabolism in plants. Phosphorus is part of many important organic compounds, including sugars-phosphates, nucleic acids and certain coenzymes. It is vital for photosynthesis and cell formation in plants and acts as a catalyst, making it easier for the plant to transfer energy. Phosphorus is also important in developing a good root system and is very mobile within the plant.

Potassium (K)

Potassium is necessary for a number of important plant functions, including the formation of sugars and starches, protein and carbohydrate synthesis and cell division. It also plays a role in adjustment of the water balance, rigidity of the plant, cold hardiness, colour enhancement and oil content of leafy crops. Potassium also plays a role in acting as a catalyst and activating or triggering a number of other plant functions.

Calcium (Ca)

Calcium is a major component of all plant cell walls and thus is important for the support of plant tissue. Calcium, once incorporated into plant tissue, is immobile so a constant supply is necessary for continued growth. Concentrations of Calcium are higher in older foliage, so it is the newer growth which first shows calcium deficiency symptoms. Calcium also plays a role in activating enzymes and regulates the flow of water movement in cells. Calcium is essential for cell growth and division and also helps to buffer when excesses of other elements are present. It is therefore an important component of a plants' root structure.

Magnesium (Mg)

Magnesium is an important structural component of the chlorophyll molecule and is thus involved in the activation and functioning of enzymes which produce sugars, carbohydrates and triglycerides. Not only is magnesium necessary for photosynthesis in plants, but it also acts as a carrier of phosphorus and is required in order to maintain ribosome structure.

Sulphur (S)

Sulphur is a component in various plant proteins, such as those which play a role in producing the flavours and odours of plants. Sulphur is also a structural component of plant amino acids, vitamins, proteins and enzymes and is necessary for chlorophyll production.

Iron (Fe)

All plants and animals require iron as an essential trace element. Both chlorophyll production, a process of photosynthesis, and the young growing parts of plants require iron. High pH levels tend to render iron unavailable to plants for uptake.

Manganese (Mn)

Manganese is directly involved in the production of oxygen from water during photosynthesis and may also be involved in chlorophyll formation. Manganese is also required for enzyme activity in photosynthesis, respiration and nitrogen metabolism.

Boron (B)

Boron is necessary for normal cell division and protein formation, as well as playing a role in cell wall construction, membrane integrity, calcium uptake and in the translocation of sugars. Boron affects at least 16 functions in plants, ranging from germination to cell division, water relationships and the movement of hormones. Boron must be available throughout the life of a plant.

Zinc (Zn)

Zinc is required for a number of plant processes. The formation of auxins (hormones which promote plant cell growth) is dependent on zinc, as is the absorption of water, and zinc also provides a source of energy for chlorophyll production. Zinc is important for carbohydrate metabolism, protein synthesis and stem growth. Low pH levels can cause zinc to become more available to the plant and thus induce a toxicity.

Copper (Cu)

Copper is concentrated in roots of plants and plays a part in nitrogen metabolism. Copper also acts as an electron carrier, as part of certain enzyme systems that use carbohydrates and proteins. High levels of copper can cause toxicity problems.

Molybdenum (Mo)

Molybdenum is a structural component of the enzyme that reduces nitrates to ammonia and is used in the formation of plant proteins. Without it, the synthesis of proteins is blocked and plant growth ceases. Nitrogen deficiency may occur if plants are lacking molybdenum.

Chlorine (Cl)

Chlorine is required for photosynthesis, where it acts as an enzyme activator during the production of oxygen from water. Chlorine is also involved in osmosis (movement of water or solutes in cells), the ionic balance necessary for plants to take up mineral elements. Chloride is the ionic form in solution which is taken up and used by plants. Some plants, such as lettuce, will show signs of toxicity if levels are too high.

Sodium (Na)

Sodium is involved in osmotic (water movement) and ionic balances in plants.

Nickel (Ni)

Nickel has just recently won the status as an essential trace element for plants. It is required for iron absorption and for seed germination. Plants grown without additional nickel will gradually reach a deficient level at about the time they mature and begin reproductive growth.

Cobalt (Co)

Cobalt is a beneficial element required in the root nodules of non legume plants.

Silicon (Si)

Silicon may not be essential for all plants, but it has been shown to be beneficial for many species. Silicon is a component of plant cell walls, so that plants with supplies of soluble silicon produce stronger, tougher cell walls, making them a mechanical barrier to piercing and sucking insects. Silicon can enhance a plant's heat and drought tolerance. Foliar sprays of silicon have been proven beneficial, by reducing populations of aphids in field crops. Tests have also found that silicon can be deposited by plants at the site of infection, to combat the penetration of the cell walls by the attacking fungus. Silicon may also improve leaf erectness and prevent or reduce toxicity symptoms from excessive levels of iron and manganese.

MINERAL DISORDERS OF LETTUCE

A well formulated, complete nutrient solution should not result in mineral deficiency symptoms in the lettuce crop. However, some conditions such as aerobic conditions around the roots caused by nutrient stagnation and lack of oxygen, can lead to problems such as iron deficiency. There is also the possibility of a nutrient salt being accidently left out of a solution formulation, or the wrong fertiliser used. A common example of this is the mistaken use of calcium ammonium nitrate, instead of calcium nitrate, which adds an unacceptable level of ammonium to the solution. It is therefore important to be able to recognise any nutritional problems in the crop as quickly as possible, and treat the cause.

A nutritional disorder is a malfunction in the physiology of a plant, resulting in abnormal growth, caused by either a deficiency or excess of a mineral element. The disorder is expressed by the plant externally and/or internally, in the form of visible symptoms. Diagnosis of a nutritional disorder involves accurate description and identification of the disorder. A deficiency or excess of each essential element causes distinct plant symptoms, which can be used to identify the disorder. It is important to detect nutritional disorders early since, as they increase in severity, the symptoms spread rapidly and may result in death of an area of plant tissue. Weaker plants will often show the first symptoms of any disorder, giving an advance warning to the grower. Lettuce is a crop which is known to be very sensitive to nutritional disorders and lettuce plants have been used as 'indicator' plants in other crops, such as tomatoes.

SPECIFIC LETTUCE MINERAL DEFICIENCY SYMPTOMS

Nitrogen (N): Older plants become restricted in growth and turn yellow-green, the oldest leaves then turn pale and die. The youngest leaves become stunted, so no heart forms in 'Butter Head' or 'Crisp Head' types. The leaves will also become smooth and tough.

Phosphorus (P): Reduced growth and failure to heart in hearting types. No other symptoms, but older leaves may present a somewhat dull or bronzed appearance. Leaf analysis is the most reliable guide to Phosphorus deficiency.

Potassium (K): Older leaves will show severe marginal and interveinal scorch (dry, brown areas).

Sulphur (S): Stunting and rosetting. Leaves, especially young ones, small stiff and pale, yellowish green, giving a rosetted appearance and causing severe stunting.

Calcium (Ca): Puckering and necrosis of young leaf margins, and sometimes death of the growing point. Tipburn like symptoms.

Magnesium (Mg): Chlorotic marbling of older leaves, which can be confused with virus infections; virus causes brittle leaves, whereas Magnesium-deficient leaves remain pliable.

Zinc (Zn): Papery necrotic areas with dark margins between the veins on older leaves.

Copper (Cu): Elongated cupped leaves; edges chlorotic and curl downwards. Plants stunted, no heads form.

Boron (B): Similar to Ca deficiency, but tip necrosis becomes worse near the growing point which may be quite blackened; young leaves deformed with prominent mid ribs.

Molybdenum (Mo): Young plants pale green, leaf margins turn brownish yellow and whither. Older plants show translucent spots, which become necrotic and coalesce. Oldest leaves affected first. Growth very stunted and plants may collapse entirely.

Manganese (Mn): Whole plant pale, especially older leaves. Later irregular pale yellow margins in older leaves, with sharp boundaries to rest of leaf. Interveinal grey-brown necrotic spotting on older leaves.

Chloride (Cl): Symptoms include wilting, stubby roots, chlorosis (yellowing) and bronzing. Odours in some plants may be decreased.

Cobalt (Co): Lack of cobalt results in nitrogen deficiency symptoms.

LETTUCE MINERAL TOXICITY SYMPTOMS

Manganese (Mn): Toxicity - irregular pale yellow margins to older leaves, sharply demarcated from rest of the leaf, which stays green.

Boron (B): Toxicity - regular yellow leaf margins in young plants. Older plants may have brown-grey sunken spots which develop in a ring-shaped pattern, veins dark brown, leaves become papery.

Chloride (Cl): Toxicity - marginal scorch in wrapper leaves.

Sodium (Na): Toxicity - will often show as wilting of the leaves before any further damage occurs. More severe toxicity symptoms include marginal tipburn, and the leaves developing a tough, 'leathery' texture.

Iron (Fe): Toxicity - while iron rarely causes toxicity problems on its own, it can lead to the plants suffering from manganese deficiency, which is induced by high levels of iron.

NUTRIENT SOLUTIONS

Many different hydroponic nutrient formulations have been published, but they are all quite similar, differing mostly in their ratio of Nitrogen (N) to Potassium (K). The differing levels of Nitrogen (N) to Potassium (K) in most solutions, is due to the fact that vegetative plants such as lettuce require more Nitrogen (N) than fruiting plants such as tomatoes, which require higher Potassium (K) rates for fruit growth and quality. Plants also need less Nitrogen (N) during short or dark days and more during long days, bright sunlight and higher temperatures. There can be a significant difference in the cost, purity and solubility of the chemicals comprising a nutrient solution, depending on the grade used. Smaller operators often buy ready mixed nutrient formulations. Larger growers prepare their own solutions to standard or slightly modified formulae.

LETTUCE FORMULATIONS AND NUTRIENT LEVEL RECOMMENDATIONS

There are many different formulations for lettuce production, and most provide a good level of all essential elements. The range of nutrient concentrations used by different growers is from 100ppm - 200ppm Nitrogen (N), 15-90ppm Phosphorus (P), 80-350 ppm Potassium (K), 122 - 220 ppm Calicum (Ca), 26 -96 ppm Magnesium (Mg), with trace elements 5 - 10ppm Iron (Fe), 0.5 - 1.0 ppm Manganese (Mn), 0.5 -2.5 ppm Zinc (Zn), 0.1 - 1.0 ppm Copper (Cu), 0.4 - 1.5ppm Boron (B), 0.5 - 1.0ppm Molybdenum (Mo).

It is important that the nutrient solution formulation be tailored to the water source, so that elements which may cause toxicities because of their presence in the water, can be left out of the nutrient mix. Using these nutrient concentration ranges, the following is a formulation used on commercial lettuce crops in New Zealand. This formulation may be adjusted for season, providing more potassium in summer to assist coloration of red varieties.

Table 2 *New Zealand Lettuce Formulation (Suntec Hydroponics, 1996).*

Summer Formulation for soft water (rain water)

Fertiliser compound	Grams to add to 100 litres of stock solution
Stock Solution A	
Calcium Nitrate	7549
Iron EDTA	260
Stock Solution B	
Potassium Nitrate	1703
MonoPotassium Phosphate	1198
Magnesium Sulphate	2571
Copper sulphate	2
Manganese Sulphate	41.7
Zinc Sulphate	2.6
Boric Acid	25.00
Ammonium Molybdate	1.02

When diluted 1 in 100, this formula gives a conductivity of 12 (EC 1.2 mS/cm) and results in parts per million (ppm) of: N = 140.9, K = 96.4, P = 25.2, Ca = 151, Mg = 25.3, S = 33.3, Fe = 2.50, Mn = 1.0, Zn = 0.06, B = 0.45, Cu = 0.05, Mo = 0.05.

The resulting Potassium to Nitrogen ratio is 0.68, the Calcium to Nitrogen ratio is 1.07, the Phosphorus to Potassium ratio is 0.26 and the Magnesium to Phosphorus ratio is 1.00.

ADDITION OF 'BENEFICIAL ELEMENTS'

Of all the 'beneficial elements', Silicon (Si) is the only element which may have some merit for hydroponic lettuce production, due to its beneficial role in resisting pest and disease attack. Researchers have found that addition of the element Silicon (Si) to hydroponic solutions reduced powdery mildew attack in cucumbers, and increased the growth and fruit production of strawberry plants.

The Dutch have used silicon in the nutrient solution for some crops since the late 1980's. Silicon in the form of potassium meta-silicate, K_2SiO_3, is added to a level of 21 ppm Si (equivalent to 45ppm SiO_2), for crops such as cucumbers, melons and lettuce. Silicon must be kept as a separate stock solution, to avoid precipitation with other elements in the concentrated form. One organic form of silicon is contained in a source called 'Pyro Clay', which is 60% silicon and contains traces of a wide range of other elements. Pyro Clay is a natural volcanic product mined in America and can be used dissolved in NFT hydroponic nutrient solutions, or as a foliar spray.

The addition of silicon to the nutrient solution has been shown to reduce the leaf coverage area of powdery mildew colonies by up to 98%, with optimum disease control occurring at 100ppm SiO_2, or higher. Foliar applications of silicon have also been shown to influence powdery mildew severity, when leaves were treated with sprays containing 1000ppm SiO_2 or more.

Silicon works in disease control by enhancing the plants' resistance to infection. Silicon accumulates around the points of infection of the pathogen and results in an increase in the development of plant resistance compounds. With foliar sprays, the high concentration of silicon on the leaf surface, acts as a physical barrier to the infection process.

Silicon may be present in some water supplies, as impurities in nutrient fertilisers, or may possibly come from such growing media as rockwool, which is made from molten silicon-containing rock. However, these levels are usually extremely low and of little value.

Many of the other 'beneficial elements', such as Selenium (Se), and Cobalt (Co), are not usually added to the nutrient solution in the form of a salt, since they are required in extremely small amounts. Most of these find their way into hydroponic nutrient by means of impurities in the major salts, or by being present in the water supply.

NUTRIENT CONDUCTIVITY (CF or EC) AND pH IMPLICATIONS

Nutrient solution pH range is from 5.5 to 6.1. Conductivity recommendations range upwards from CF 7 (EC 0.7 mS/cm), but best success is reported to occur at CF 12 - 22 (EC 1.2 - 2.2 mS/cm). The incidence of tipburn is said to be increased by high solution conductivity (EC). A CF of 10 (1.0 mS/cm) has been recommended during propagation. The range of nutrient concentrations used by different researchers is from 100ppm to 200ppm Nitrogen (N), 15-90ppm Phosphorus (P), 80-350 ppm Potassium (K), 122-320 ppm Calcium (Ca), 26-96 ppm Magnesium (Mg), all with the usual trace element concentrations.

Many researchers have investigated the effect of solution conductivity (EC) on lettuce growth and development. Trials carried out on 'Butter Head' and 'Cos' lettuce with EC ranges from 1.5 - 5.0 mS/cm (15 - 50 CF) have been evaluated and it was found that for both cultivars, the overall effect of solution conductivity on shoot fresh weight was minor. Increased conductivity resulted in increased root dry weight. It was also noted that the plants grown at the high EC levels (4.0 to 5.0 mS/cm) had less water content and their texture was rather 'leathery', compared to the other treatment plants. It was also suggested that plants growing at the lower EC values were less resistant to veinal tipburn. The conclusion was that, although lettuce plants can be grown over a wide range of solution conductivities, EC levels within the range 2.0 - 3.0 mS/cm (CF 20 - 30) give the more satisfactory results *(Economakis, 1990)*.

In a recent study on the effects of conductivity on lettuce yields and quality, it was found that increasing the solution conductivity from EC 0.5 to 2.0 mS/cm (5 to 20 CF), resulted in increased lettuce total dry weight, especially in the red sails and oak leaf cultivars. However, at the higher solution conductivity, the 'Butter Head' and some 'Oak Leaf' showed the physiological condition tipburn. Lettuce breeding has been intensive in recent times, and many of the newer cultivars are adapted for high nutrition and rapid growth, however, Australian research currently recommends a solution conductivity EC of 1.0 to 1.6 mS/cm (CF 10 - 16) for lettuce growth, with EC 0.4 - 0.6 mS/cm (4 to 6 CF) in summer to avoid tipburn.

HYDROPONIC SOLUTION FLOW RATES

A commonly recommended flow rate for hydroponic NFT lettuce is approx 1.2 litres/minute, although this is dependent on the gully width. A recent New Zealand study found that increasing the flow rate from 2 to 12 litres/min had a negative effect on lettuce growth, with the optimum range being 2 to 6 litres/min *(Care, 1994)*. Although plants are presented with more nutrients per unit time at higher flow rates, the reduction in growth and nutrient uptake may be a result of physical damage to the root system.

DISSOLVED OXYGEN

The root system of a plant needs oxygen, if it is to remain in a healthy growing condition. A plant's basic requirement for oxygen is not fixed at any particular minimum level, but varies according to the temperature conditions. The warmer the growing conditions, the more oxygen is necessary for good growth, due to higher rates of respiration.

Plants obtain their supplies of oxygen from various sources, some from the atmosphere and some from that dissolved in the nutrient solution. Without an adequate supply of oxygen, it is impossible for the oxidation of organic substances in respiration to take place. Exclusion of oxygen in the root zone interferes with the respiration of the protoplasm of the root cells, causing its death and consequent failure of the absorbing mechanism. Progressive wilting of the shoots and leaves follows. Waterlogging is the chief cause of a lack of oxygen supply in hydroponics.

Lettuce will grow satisfactorily at a dissolved oxygen level of at least 4ppm. The absence of oxygen in the nutrient solution will stop the process of root respiration and seriously damage and kill the plants. The content of dissolved oxygen in a nutrient solution has been shown to decrease from 6.7 to 2.7 ppm O_2 over a 7.6m channel length. In another trial, dissolved oxygen only decreased in saturation by 2% over a 3m channel length. These differences may be due to the different types of crops grown (cucumbers vs lettuce) and differing flow rates. Oxygen can be introduced into a system in a number of ways, the most popular being the fall of the returning solution back into the holding tank. The greater the fall of the solution, the more oxygen will be forced into the solution.

CHAPTER ⑧ - PESTS, DISEASES & PHYSIOLOGICAL PROBLEMS

CHAPTER (8) - PESTS, DISEASES & PHYSIOLOGICAL PROBLEMS

PESTS AND DISEASES

Pests and disease control is largely a matter of taking the right preventative measures. Because of the shape and close spacing of hydroponic lettuce, it is virtually impossible to effectively act against a disease once it is established. Mainly because of the short time it takes for it to mature, the crop is potentially trouble-free.

PESTS - IDENTIFICATION AND CONTROL

Aphids

Aphids are a common pest of greenhouse lettuce and are most easily controlled by chemical sprays. They are often difficult to detect on lettuce crops, unless the underside of the leaves is closely examined. Under heavy aphid infestations, lettuce leaves may become curled and blistered and plant growth is checked - these pests are also vectors of virus diseases. Aphid species infecting lettuce crops can range in colour from yellow, to brown, green or black, and are small, soft bodied with long thin legs *(Figure 12)*. Aphids are common in warmer conditions such as early spring or autumn, but are not usually a problem in mid winter. High numbers of aphids can stunt seedlings or young plants, but rarely cause economic losses in older plants. The main problem with aphid infestations is that they contaminate harvested plants, making them unsaleable. Aphids are easily controlled by spraying once an infestation is detected. Many products control aphids including Orthene, Attack, Lannate, and Maldison.

Figure 12. Aphid - Wingless Adult

Caterpillars

Caterpillars can also affect lettuce crops and can be controlled by spraying with a suitable insecticide such as Carbaryl, Orthene, Maldison, Lannate or Attack. Continuing checks on the crop with spot sprays where necessary should be adequate in most cases.

Slugs and Snails

Slugs and snails can be a problem and are best controlled by the use of slug baits, applied immediately after planting. Slugs and snails are rarely a problem on bench hydroponic systems, but can cause rapid destruction of seedlings in the propagation house under wet and humid conditions.

Whitefly

Whitefly can become a serious pest in greenhouse lettuce crops, particularly over the summer months. The adults of the whitefly are the stage which is most easily recognised. They are tiny (about 1.5mm) white moth-like insects, which fly up from the undersides of the crop leaves when disturbed. Whitefly lay their eggs on the undersides of the leaves. These eggs are bullet shaped, protrude out from the leaf surface and are too small (0.2mm) to be seen with the unaided eye. The colour is milky white, which turns to black just before hatching. The next stage after hatching is the 'crawler', which usually settles on the same leaf on which it hatched. On settling, the crawler stage moults and from then on is in the form of a semi-transparent 'scale'. The piercing mouth parts of the white fly adults and juvenile scale become embedded in the leaf, from which they draw nourishment. The scale stage moults a further two times before the adult insect emerges *(Figure 13)*.

Whitefly require living plants in order to sustain a population, but the mature scales can survive for several weeks on dead plant tissue. The source of infestation can be from either inside or outside the greenhouse: adults can fly in from outside, if no scale are present inside. All stages of whitefly can overwinter on suitable plants, so there is no complete break in the life-cycle during the winter months. As a result of whitefly feeding on the crop, honeydew, a sticky sugary solution, is produced by all stages except the eggs. This coats the leaf surfaces and sooty mould (a black mould) grows on the honeydew under high humidity conditions. While sooty mould causes no direct injury, excessive levels can interfere with photosynthesis and contaminate the crop.

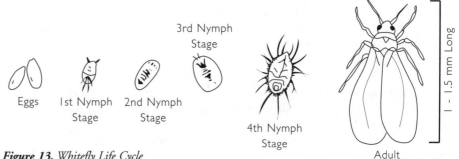

Figure 13. *Whitefly Life Cycle*

Whitefly Control

Most insecticides kill only adults, but some also kill eggs, crawlers and early scales. For insecticides that affect only adults, several repeat treatments at 3 - 5 day intervals are required to achieve control. There is great potential for whitefly to develop resistance to insecticides. In many countries, whitefly are known to be resistant to all major classes of insecticide. It is recommended that insecticides are not applied unnecessarily and that more than one type of insecticide is used, to prevent resistant populations becoming established. Suitable insecticides include Attack, Lannate, Dichlorvos, and Orthene - care must be taken with these sprays as they contain synthetic pyrethroid and organophosphates. Addition of mineral oil or detergent may help with coverage of the spray, however, whitefly do rapidly develop resistance to these pesticides.

Other methods of control now involve integrated pest management (IPM) techniques, involving a small parasitic wasp *Encarsia formosa* (marketed under the name 'Enforce'). This whitefly parasite is tiny, and black and yellow in colour. The female wasp flies to whitefly infested plants and searches for whitefly nymphs, into which she lays an egg. The parasitised whitefly nymph grows to full size before it is killed by the parasite larva. At this stage, the scale turns black so that it is easy to recognise parasitised whitefly. When the larval parasite has fully grown and changed into the wasp, it cuts a hole in the black scale and sets off to infect another whitefly. Producers of the parasites send them to the growers at the black scale size. The main criterion for successful use of *E. formosa* is that there must be very few whitefly in the crop at the time the parasite introductions start. This is because it takes two months for the parasite to become established and another month to substantially reduce the whitefly population.

Other methods used to control whitefly include yellow sticky traps, which help remove excess whitefly, and the use of natural pesticides such as those derived from the 'neem' plant. Neem acts to disrupt the formation of the whitefly exoskeleton, thus reducing population numbers. A complete clean out of the greenhouse, with removal of all dead plant material at least once a year, will help to control whitefly populations.

Top: Symptoms of fungus gnat infestation on a red variety of lettuce in an NFT system.
Bottom: Advanced symptoms of fungus gnat damage, including secondary infection by fungal disease

Fungus Gnats

Fungus gnats are a species of fly resembling sandflies or 'midges'. They cause damage during the propagation and planting stages, by laying eggs onto damp media at the base of the lettuce plant. The maggots which hatch from these eggs migrate into the media and begin to feed on the developing roots, causing direct damage to the plant and allowing infection by opportunist fungi such as pythium. Symptoms of fungus gnat attack include wilting and yellowing of the lower leaves, while the root system will appear severely restricted and brown in colour, and the plant may come away from the pot at the base of the stem.

   The maggots will be seen in the media - they are 3 - 4 mm long, clear with a black head and grey colouring visible inside. Control is best achieved by avoiding over watering, although even dry media can be invaded by fungus gnats. Granular insecticides such as Phorate or disyston incorporated into the seed sowing media are the most effective chemical treatment for fungus gnats. However, these chemicals are very toxic and persistent.

Birds

Birds are known to attack lettuce seedlings at certain times of the year. Sparrows seem to be the most common problem, often feeding on newly planted seedlings in outdoor systems. Sparrows have also been known to damage hearted lettuce at maturity, by picking holes in the leaves. Birds may be controlled by repellent bait such as Mesurol, which is sprayed over the seedlings and acts as a repellent due to its offensive taste. Bird scaring devices may also be used - reflective foil tape stretched along the system beds helps to scare away birds when it moves in the breeze.

Thrips

Thrips are small insects and easily overlooked. They are slender, with two pairs of long strap-like wings with few veins and fringed with long hairs However, some species are wingless. Symptoms of thrip damage include small silvery flecks on the plant surface, which eventually coalesce giving a bleached appearance. In addition, there is often distortion of growth in response to the insect's injected saliva. Thrips are not a common problem on lettuce, but do infect a number of greenhouse crops. Control is with the use of chemical sprays such as Maldison.

Mites

Mites can become a problem in greenhouses when warm, dry conditions prevail. The two spotted mite and red spider mite are extremely small (0.3 - 0.5mm) and can barely be seen with the unaided eye. As with whitefly, they occur primarily on the undersides of leaves where the eggs are also laid, and hibernating females can survive for months. The host range for mites is very wide and includes many cultivated plants and weed species.

   The damage caused by mites is primarily indirect, through reduction of leaf action. Symptoms include a yellowing, followed by bronzed appearance of heavily infested plants. Fine webbing may be seen on the undersides of leaves. Mites have developed a high resistance to a number of insecticides/miticides and sprays should not be used unnecessarily. Suitable control products include Mavrick[R] or Dicofol, the effectiveness of which can be increased with the addition of a mineral oil for added coverage. Integrated pest management (IPM) methods can also be used on mites. The predatory mite, *Phytoseiulus persimilis* is a predator of the two spotted mite. This is a red, shiny, fast moving mite with an enormous appetite for its prey and the added advantage of breeding twice as fast as the pest. Predatory mite populations are purchased on bean leaves and introduced into the crop.

Leaf Miners

Leaf miners occasionally cause damage to lettuce seedlings, or the foliage of mature crops. The leaf miner larvae hatch 2 - 4 days after the eggs are laid by the adult flies, and begin mining between the upper and lower surfaces of the leaves. The winding, whitish tunnels they create are initially narrow, but they increase in width as the larvae grow. Larvae emerge from the 'leafmines' after completing three instars and pupate on the leaf surfaces. Adult flies emerge from the pupae after 8 - 11 days. Leaf miners can be controlled with systemic insecticides such as Orthene, since contact sprays cannot harm the larvae under the leaf epidermis.

LETTUCE DISEASES - IDENTIFICATION AND CONTROL

Pythium

(See 'Seed Raising' section for Pythium control during seedling development). Pythium is present in nearly all hydroponic systems. It comes in from the water supply, or from the surrounding vegetation. However, pythium should not cause problems in a healthy, well grown crop. This disease only infects plants through sites of damage, such as root injury caused during transplanting, or by mineral toxicities, nutrient stagnation, or excessive temperatures. Pythium will only cause problems on healthy plants if there is an active source of spore production within the system, when the spore population becomes high. The signs of pythium damage include an initial browning of the root tips, which in advanced cases turns black and rots. Pythium infections usually mean the system must be shut down, and thoroughly cleaned with a strong bleach (sodium hypochloride solution), including all tanks, gullies, pipes, and pumps. Another way of controlling pythium may be to prevent spore population explosions by first sterilising the water source, or sterilisation of the nutrient solution with either UV light or ozone injection.

The best preventative measure against pythium attack is a healthy, rapidly growing plant, as pythium is an opportunist pathogen and will enter at the site of tissue injury, or if the plants are overly succulent or weakened/stressed for some reason. Pythium needs a plant pathologist to formally identify the pathogen, and it is a good idea to have any potential water source (particularly dams and ground water) tested for pythium levels if this is a suspected source of severe infection.

Downy Mildew *(Bremia lactucae)*

Downy mildew on seedlings and small plants can be devastating, but is controlled by spraying with Zineb, Maneb, Mancozeb or Metalaxyl. This fungus can render mature plants unsaleable through the unsightly yellow lesions on the leaves. The disease is encouraged by warm moist conditions. Plants suffering a growth check are predisposed to downy mildew. Spray preventatively in the early stages of the crop with Bravo or Mancozeb and where possible grow resistant cultivars. On older plants, the symptoms are small areas on the leaves of a paler green, which becomes yellow. Underneath, the typical white, fluffy growth can be seen. The high humidity conditions which are common in autumn favour rapid spread. Also, in autumn there is a supply of airborne spores from outdoor lettuce crops, but these spores only germinate if there is a film of water on the leaf. If the plants wilt, or are put under other stress, development of the fungus is favoured.

Sclerotinia *(Sclerotinia sclerotiorum)*

Sclerotinia is a soft rot in which, at a later stage, the 'sclerotia' (black granules) can be seen developing on the lower part of the stem. It causes the whole plant to collapse in time. Removal and disposal of affected plants is advisable, to lower future incidence of the disease.

Sclerotinia appears when conditions are warm, in early autumn and late spring crops. Plants affected collapse and a soft rot is found at the base of the stem. White fluffy growth develops on the rot and later large, black resting bodies (sclerotia) about the size of an onion seed develop. These drop off into the ground and are resistant to chemical sterilants and will infect the following crop. Careful removal and disposal, by burning or burying of all infected plants, limits the spread, and early detection limits damage. Chemical control of the white fluffy fungus is possible using Benonyl or Ronilan.

Botrytis *(Botrytis cineria)*

This is the most common and the most destructive fungal disease of lettuce and accounts for a large proportion of total crop losses. The spores are always present in the air, but only infect the lettuce plant through physical wounds, or lesions caused by other diseases. As with sclerotinia, the stem may rot through at the base, causing collapse of the plant. Cold and damp conditions favour its spread. Preventative spraying with a protectant fungicide such as Thiram will provide a fair measure of protection.

Internal Soft Rot *(Erwinia carotovora).*

This disease is occasionally troublesome and most often appears on headed lettuce when the weather is warm and humid. The disease occurs between the tightly folded heart leaves and is difficult to detect, even during harvest. Once infected, it is impossible to get a good coverage with sprays. Control is possible by spraying with a copper fungicide when conditions are conducive to the disease, so it is important to be able to recognise these conditions. Selection of less susceptible varieties will help.

LETTUCE RINGSPOT (Anthracnose)

Ringspot (or anthracnose) of lettuce is caused by the fungus *Microdochium panattonianum,* and has increased in severity in lettuce crops over recent years. The first visible signs of ringspot disease are small, yellowish-brown spots on leaves (usually on the undersurface) that merge into larger, irregular, brown patches of dead tissue, which in time falls out giving the plants a ragged 'shot hole' appearance. Lesions on the mid-ribs are usually oval shaped and markedly sunken.

The major source of *M. panattonianum* inoculum appears to be infected plant debris from previous crops. Control of weeds outside the greenhouse or around the growing area will also minimize the risk of infection. Under field conditions in Victoria, Australia, the fungus has been shown to survive on infected lettuce debris for up to 20 weeks. Wet conditions are conducive to the production of spores, which are dispersed by water-splash or wind-blown rain and serve to spread the disease from plant to plant. Spores of *M. panattonianum* are reported to germinate at temperatures between 3-26°C, but not in the absence of free water. Optimum infections occur following leaf wetness periods of over 8 hours, at temperatures around 15°C. Under glasshouse conditions, Bravo and Captan are the most effective fungicides for the control of ringspot on lettuce *(Broadhurst and Wood, 1996).*

BACTERIAL INFECTIONS

Bacterial leaf infections can be a problem when moisture is allowed to sit on the leaves. Copper sprays offer the best protection from bacterial problems.

LETTUCE VIRUSES

Lettuce Mosaic Virus

Although widespread in outdoor lettuce, infection under cover is not often seen. Symptoms are a mottling of the leaf, with pale green or yellowish areas among the darker green of the rest of the leaf. Young plants are most affected, becoming stunted and failing to heart in the Butter Head types. The viruses can be seed carried (although many varieties are now virus-indexed and virus-free), and this is often the primary source of infection.

Top: Botrytis infection on an outdoor grown 'Crisp Head' variety.
Bottom: Advanced Botrytis infection on an outdoor grown, green loose leaf variety.

Weeds such as groundsel and sow-thistle are also infected and become an infection source. This virus is mainly transmitted by aphids. Control is firstly by ensuring clean seed and destroying any infected seedlings and plants, and secondly by controlling aphids with insecticides, both in the propagation area and growing beds.

Cucumber Mosaic Virus

This is the commonest plant virus known, infecting many vegetables, flowers and weeds. It is not carried by lettuce seed, but may be carried by the seeds of common chickweed, hence control of weeds is important. Symptoms are very similar to lettuce mosaic, although there is usually a more yellowish mottle and sometimes necrotic spotting. It is also spread by aphids.

Big Vein Virus

This has all the signs of a virus, but virus particles have never been found in infected plants. Symptoms are a widening of the leaf veins, caused by the production of a band of light green to colourless cells on either side of the vein. Affected lettuce are slower growing, may be distorted in shape and often have a bitter flavour.

PHYSIOLOGICAL DISORDERS

Tipburn of Lettuce Plants

Tipburn is a physiological disorder affecting the margins of the leaves, and is especially serious when leaf margins within the heart are affected. The affected margins become necrotic and dry. With both normal tipburn and marginal tipburn, part of the leaf wilts and dries up. The damage is caused when leaves are losing water into the air faster than their roots can take it up, or, when there is high humidity and little water lost, the transpiration stream in which the calcium is transported is restricted, and thus tipburn occurs. Most tipburn is seen when the crop is near to harvest in late winter and spring.

There are other causes of tipburn which should not be confused with that induced by the low calcium distribution in plants. These include frost damage, windburn from strong winds, herbicide injury, salt spray burn and excessively high nutrient solution conductivities.

This disorder is caused by a shortage of calcium in the expanding leaves. This can be the result of high humidity conditions, or water stress caused by a high conductivity nutrient solution. Transpiration of the expanding leaves within the head is limited by surrounding leaves, especially under high humidity conditions, and tipburn can be severe in crops being allowed to stand too long before cutting.

With normal cases of tipburn, the younger heart leaves wilt and the cells at the edge are killed. With marginal tipburn, the older leaves are affected, but since the air circulation is better, the tissue usually dries up and leaves a scorched appearance along the edges of the leaf. The main causes of conditions favourable to tipburn can be listed as follows:

- High temperatures during sunny weather

- Hot, drying winds

- High conductivity (EC) of the nutrient solution

- Poor root system due to inadequate oxygenation or root death

Numerous investigations with field and greenhouse-grown lettuce have indicated the relationship between temperature, light intensity and duration, and relative humidity on tipburn. No relationship has been found between solution Potassium (K), Sodium (Na) or pH levels and the occurrence of tipburn in hydroponic lettuce. The general conclusion of numerous researchers is that tipburn injury is primarily controlled by genetic factors (i.e cultivar selection) and is influenced by environmental conditions maintained during growth, with greater incidence of tipburn observed in greenhouse experiments conducted during the long, warm days of spring and summer *(Bres and Weston, 1991)*.

Calcium (Ca) and Tipburn

Calcium is taken up by young regions of plant roots and this uptake can be antagonised by other cations, such as Potassium (K) and Ammonium (NH4). Calcium moves around in the xylem; it is a relatively immobile element, generally following the transpirational flow of water. Thus, calcium moves less readily to organs with low rates of transpiration, such as fruits and the tips of enclosed, rapidly expanding leaves in lettuce, than it does to actively transpiring leaves. This is why calcium deficiency disorders tend to occur in fruits and leaf tips. Thus tipburn is a calcium transport problem, not a calcium supply problem. So although adequate calcium may be present in the nutrient solution, its uptake and distribution under certain environmental conditions will not be sufficient to prevent tipburn in susceptible cultivars.

The problem appears to become more serious with lettuce as the crop nears maturity, and can cause heavy losses. The reason appears to be that as the heads tighten (in heading varieties which are more susceptible to tipburn), there is less air flow through the heads, and water use by the inner leaves slows down, leading to lower calcium levels in those leaves. The humidity around the leaves increases and if bacteria are present, a rot develops on the dead leaf tip. In warm summer conditions on lettuce, this develops rapidly as 'slime', either in the greenhouse or in the market chain.

Overseas, several different types of tipburn in lettuce are recognised. Dry tipburn occurs in soil grown crops, when the growing medium is dry and the roots cannot supply water and calcium rapidly enough. There is also normal tipburn, which occurs with the rapid change of weather, veinal tipburn, which develops with the tight heads and high humidity in the head, and a latex tipburn which develops if the plant is going to develop a seed head. To some extent, low levels of Magnesium (Mg) and Boron (B) can cause tipburn in lettuce, and should be checked if there is a persistent problem not fitting the usual causes above. There is no cure once tipburn is noted on lettuce, but the extent of tipburn can be minimised by observing the following practices:

• Ensuring adequate solution Calcium (Ca) levels;

• Avoiding excessive Potassium (K) and Nitrogen (N) levels;

• Using the nitrate form of Nitrogen in preference to the ammonium form;

• Using Calcium sprays during mid-growth stages, or when required.

Recently, researchers have looked at methods which may reduce the severity of tipburn in hydroponic lettuce. It has been suggested that circulation of either straight water or calcium nitrate solution (100mg Ca/litre) at night only, may be a commercially acceptable means of reducing tipburn losses in lettuce crops grown using hydroponics *(Cresswell, 1991)*. In this experiment, plants were grown in a glasshouse using NFT and during the day received a complete nutrient solution (EC 2 mS/cm). At night, other treatments were imposed - these included a complete nutrient solution, tap water, or calcium nitrate solution containing either 100mg/litre or 200mg/litre of calcium. Tipburn occurred in the control and its incidence was reduced by the other treatments. This effect was associated with an increase in the concentration of calcium in new leaves, except in the water treatment.

Top: Tipburn symptoms on the newer leaves of an outdoor grown Oak leaf cultivar
Bottom: Marginal tipburn on the older leaves of an over mature, greenhouse grown 'Butter Head' cultivar

Other researchers have reported a correlation between nutrient solution conductivity (EC) and the incidence of tipburn in hydroponic lettuce crops. The number of leaves per plant with tipburn was found to be reduced from 23.1 to 4.4 as the EC was reduced from 3.6 to 0.4 mS/cm.

Glassiness

A problem arising in lettuce production is 'glassiness' or veinal tipburn, a physiological disorder caused by excessive water uptake in relation to the transpiration loss by the plant. Glassiness is stimulated by factors which inhibit transpiration and those which promote water uptake. Tissues become water soaked and translucent in this disorder, which occurs mainly in the winter. Leaves can recover from mild symptoms, but in severe cases the leaves develop necrotic areas. It is caused by excessive water uptake and limited transpiration. This occurs under dull humid conditions.

Wilting

Crop wilting may occur during the middle of the day during warm conditions, when the leaves are transpiring more water than the root system can take up. Lowering the conductivity will assist with water uptake, but the leaves will regain turgidity as the temperatures drop later in the day. By dawn, plants should have regained full turgidity. Shading of the crop will lower air temperatures and lessen the degree of wilting experienced.

Wilting can be caused by a number of other problems, including excessive conductivity (EC) levels, various pest and disease problems, or inadequate oxygen caused by stagnation of the solution.

SPRAYING FOR PEST AND DISEASE CONTROL AND SANITATION

Prevention of pest and disease problems can be assisted by attention to correct sanitation procedures during cropping and after harvest. All crop residue, such as old leaves and dead or diseased plants, should be removed from the cropping area and destroyed as soon as possible, since these tend to harbour pest and disease organisms. After harvest, the system and gullies should be wiped down with a 10% sodium hypochloride solution (i.e household bleach) or chlorine solution, and thoroughly rinsed. All seedling propagation equipment should also be cleaned after use. Once a year, it is recommended that the entire system be disinfected by running a chlorine solution over a period of 24 hours, followed by several rinses of water. However, in many operations where there is continual year round cropping, this type of system sanitation is not practical.

When it is necessary to spray for a pest or disease outbreak, it is important to follow the manufacturer's recommendations for the product used. Particular attention should be paid to the concentration and compatibility of different chemicals, as tender lettuce leaves are extremely susceptible to spray damage caused by careless application. For example, some sprays cannot be mixed and applied at the same time - copper is one which should not be mixed with fungicides such as Thiram, and can cause damage to young foliage.

Many of the pesticides used on lettuce crops contain organo-phosphates or synthetic pyrethroids, both of which are extremely toxic to humans, so protective clothing and respirators must be worn and regularly maintained. Protective clothing is important, since many chemicals can be absorbed into the body through the skin, resulting in poisoning. Contaminated clothing should be washed separately from the general wash to avoid cross-contamination.

When working with the liquid concentrates, there is often a danger of splash to the eyes. Simple goggles or a face shield will protect against this *(NZ Agrichemical Manual)*. Use of a cartridge or canister-type respirator will also be required for spray application, to protect against inhaling chemical spray vapours. Cartridges or canisters from the respirator need to be changed after eight hours use, or immediately if you can smell the pesticide through your mask *(NZ Agrichemical Manual)*.

ALTERNATIVE PEST AND DISEASE CONTROL

The first line of defence in the battle against fungal, wilt and virus diseases such as downy mildew, botrytis and many others, is to select and grow cultivars which show some resistance to these diseases. Many commercial seed catalogues list the disease resistance characteristics of different lettuce cultivars.

The majority of the organic sprays used to control fungal diseases are more of a preventative measure, rather than a quick fix once the crop has become severely infected. Most 'organic' fungicide compounds act to prevent the fungal hyphae from penetrating the leaf surface and becoming established, so it is vital to monitor the plants and either spray as a preventative measure during periods when fungal diseases are likely to take hold, or at the very first sign of crop infection.

Good control of some fungal diseases can be achieved with sprays made from a combination of sodium bicarbonate and a high quality detergent. A mixture of 2 g/litre of sodium bicarbonate, with additional detergent or a commercial wetting agent, will offer some control of fungal diseases, but is most effective when used as a preventative measure. Resistance to fungal attack can sometimes be induced from within. Heathy plants with thin, smooth cuticles often repel fungal spores which cannot become established if they cannot penetrate the leaf surface. By adding an ionic surfactant to spray mixtures, the cuticle thickness of the plant leaf can be increased, thus making it even more difficult for fungal spores to take hold. One of the ways hydroponic growers have induced fungal resistance is to give the plant silica, either by adding this to the nutrient solution, or by spraying onto the leaf surface. Silica strengthens the leaf cells, making it difficult for fungal spores to penetrate and become established. A high level of calcium in the plant tissue also promotes this physical resistance to disease.

Bacterial diseases of lettuce can be controlled with streptomycin formulas. This is a natural antibiotic (microbial formulation) spray which is highly effective.

Alternative pest control methods are growing in popularity as there is an increasing demand, even in the hydroponics sector, for 'reduced chemical' produce. There are a few effective 'organic' pest control measures, although some are not as effective as many of the chemical sprays that are currently used on lettuce crops. One of the most promising substances for the control of a wide range of insect pests affecting lettuce crops is Neem oil. Neem oil is extracted from the leaves and berries of the Neem tree *(Azadirachta indica)*, which is native to India and Burma. This product has a wide range of active ingredients, which have the ability to fatally disrupt the lifecycles of a huge range of insect pests, while having no harmful effects on people, animals and beneficial insects. In tests over the last couple of decades, entomologists have found that neem materials can affect more than 200 insect species, as well as some mites, nematodes, fungi, bacteria and even a few viruses.

Organic neem sprays are unique, in that they are not outright killers. Instead, they alter an insect's behaviour until it can no longer feed or breed or metamorphose, and can cause no further crop damage. Many approved neem formulations are now available on the market in the United States, however, registration of such pesticides in some other countries is not complete yet, and they cannot be legally used on commercial food crops. However, it is only a matter of time before Neem-based insecticides come into widespread use as a 'safe' and effective means of pest control.

Pyrethrin is another plant-based insecticide, which has been scientifically proven to be an effective pesticide. Classed as a 'botanical insecticide', pyrethrin products are made from the flowers of *Chrysanthemum cinearaefolium*. Although pyrethrin is considered safer to use than insecticides such as organo-phosphates, it is still toxic to people, animals and bees, but to a lesser extent than it is to insect pests. The advantage is that these sprays cause rapid debilitation of a very wide range of insect pests and they also break down quickly in the environment.

There are some effective smothering agents for use against insect pests such as whitefly and aphids. Insecticidal soap and mineral oil sprays are examples of these types, which have some degree of control on the adult insects.

Microbial controls are also becoming increasing available. These are sprays which contain bacteria, fungi or viruses which infect certain insect pests, rapidly killing them. Microbial controls have the advantage of only affecting the insect species targeted and pose no threat to humans or animals. One of the most well known microbial controls is *Bacillus thuringensis* (known as 'BT'), a bacterial agent which is effective against a number of caterpillar species. BT leaves no harmful residue and can be used right up until the day of harvest. This agent works by producing toxins in the alkaline digestive system of *Lepidoptera* larvae and is non-toxic to other organisms.

In some countries, a microbial control agent for the greenhouse whitefly is in use. The entomopathogenic fungus, *Verticillium lecanii*, is a safe and effective control with spores which penetrate the host and develop inside the pest, killing it and eventually erupting through the skin to release more spores. A whitefly-specific strain is on the market, in the form of a wettable powder containing the fungal spores, but it is only available in selected countries.

DISCLAIMER

Chemical treatments mentioned in this chapter are suggested as a guide only. Growers should check with their local Department of Agriculture and/or relevant regulatory authotiry before applying any crop chemicals. The legality of chemical use on specific crops varies from country to country, as well as between states and territories.

CHAPTER ⑨ - HARVESTING & SHELF LIFE

CHAPTER ⑨ - HARVESTING AND SHELF LIFE

Harvesting of Lettuce Crops

Lettuce, like other green leafy vegetables are highly perishable. They are particularly susceptible to water loss after harvest. Unless proper care is taken, leafy vegetables will quickly develop a wilted appearance.

Lettuce should be harvested early in the day, while temperatures are still relatively cool and the crop turgid. Hydroponic lettuce is usually harvested with the root system intact, in order to prolong shelf life and prevent premature wilting. Large growers now often leave the small plastic pot on the root system. The root system is bundled up, the lettuce placed in a clear plastic bag or cellophane wrapper, and a rubber band used to secure the plastic around the root system. It is important that lettuce is handled with extreme care, since bruising and leaf damage can easily occur at harvest and result in browning and decay of the leaf. The bagged lettuce is then packed into cartons or plastic crates/trays for shipment to market. The cartons should hold the lettuce firmly, so that they cannot move and be damaged in transit, yet not so tightly that they are compressed and bruised.

The following simple techniques are critical to maintain the product in optimum condition and reduce the loss of shelf life which occurs at high temperatures.

- Harvest in the cool of the day.

- Pack into cool crates.

- Get harvested product into the shade as soon as possible.

- Remove the field heat as soon as possible after harvest.

- Transport in covered vehicles.

- Avoid holding product at ambient temperature.

- Cool storage facilities are critical in removing field heat. If you do not have the facilities, then the above techniques and getting to market as quickly as possible will still benefit your product.

Ethylene gas reduces vegetable quality and exposure to this gas should be avoided. Most green leaf vegetables are sensitive to ethylene and lettuce is no exception. Lettuce should be stored and transported separately from products known to produce ethylene (apples, pears, stonefruit, tomatoes, melons, bananas etc). Damaged, rotting or decaying produce also releases ethylene, so it is imperative to keep storage areas clean. Combustion engines (e.g petrol/diesel forklifts) also produce ethylene, so keep areas well ventilated and do not leave the engine running when not in use.

Most green leafy vegetables are susceptible to freezing injury. Whilst lettuce benefits from being stored at 0 - 2°C (32° - 35.6°F), freezing or chilling injury can result when the temperature drops below 0°C (32°F). The optimum conditions for short-term holding of lettuce is to store at 0 - 2°C, with a relative humidity between 90 - 98%. As with avoiding chilling injury, it is important to monitor produce temperatures and not rely on air temperature measurements. Similarly, produce should not be subjected to higher than recommended temperatures.

Lollo Bionda type (green frill/coral), lettuce in plastic sleeves, packed into returnable plastic crates destined for sale

Post Harvest Handling

Harvested lettuce is a mass of living tissue which continues to respire and lose water in transpiration, and which is subject to disease attack and to chemical and physiological deterioration. All these contribute to the gradual deterioration after harvest of the crop. Hydroponic lettuce is considered a high quality product and is thus packaged to protect and prolong its usable life. The plastic wrappers, bags or cellophane sleeves used for gourmet lettuce, protects the produce from mechanical damage, helps retain moisture and in some cases, such as with the fresh cut salad packs, allows a modified atmosphere inside the package which further prolongs shelf life and maintains quality.

Prevention of water loss is a major advantage of consumer packaging when moisture retentive films are used. The shelf life of packaged produce is lengthened over non-packaged produce. Leafy vegetables keep best under a relative humidity of 90 to 95%, as this minimises wilting. Within a film package, the humidity rapidly builds up and may approach or reach 100%. It is usually desirable to perforate film packages for lettuce, to provide ventilation and facilitate gas exchange.

Cooling and Refrigeration

Refrigeration at the optimum temperature for the produce, combined with high humidity, is the best method of extending storage or shelf life. Refrigeration controls the growth of many decay-producing bacteria and fungi, and slows metabolism. Refrigeration effectively retards respiration, which is usually desirable.

Lettuce must be kept cool after harvest. Quick removal of field heat prolongs the life of the lettuce. Vacuum cooling is popular, as this allows the lettuce to be pre-cooled to about 1°C within about 20 minutes. Growers with cool stores should cool their lettuce as quickly as possible, and forced-air cooling is recommended for this. Forced-air cooling draws cool-store air through stacks of perforated cartons which contain the produce. Cooling time with forced-air cooling is about 3 hours. 'Butter Head' lettuce will hold in cool store at 0 - 2°C for up to about three weeks, with no discernable loss of quality.

Modified Atmosphere Packaging for Fresh-Cut Produce

Fresh-cut, pre-prepared salad packs which are used for products such as lettuce are designed to bring convenience food which is top quality and fresh, to the consumer who doesn't want to fiddle around cutting and washing the leaves. Prepacked lettuce leaf mixtures are either packed in sealed plastic bags, or in punnets with all-in-one lids. Often these mixes have about eight attractively set out vegetables in a clear plastic punnet, sometimes with a sachet of salad dressing included.

France was one of the early leaders in the development of convenience packaged salads, and some of the largest vegetable growers in the United Kingdom have established 'on-farm' preparation and packing operations, to produce salad packs for supermarket chains such as Marks and Spencer. Fresh-cut has now also become big business in the US, with new products and mixes appearing at the rate of approximately one per week. Fresh-cut items are the fastest growing sector in American supermarkets and this component of fresh produce has become so specialised that it now has its own trade magazine, 'Fresh Cut', which is published 12 times a year.

The appeal of fresh-cut salad packs is due to a number of factors including:

- Quality - Fresh-cut mixes are of the very highest quality, with taste being the most important component. The mixes are marketed in transparent packages, which enable customers to see the quality.

- Convenience - Fresh-cut salads, vegetables and fruit mixes are instantly usable, without the need for time-consuming preparation and without causing waste.

- Labour savings for food service and retailers - Labour costs are high in stores and food service outlets at US $14 to $16 per hour, and pre-prepared fresh-cut produce reduces labour requirements greatly.

- Ease of Display - Attention required in retail stores is much less than for loose produce, which requires continual inspection and spraying. Restaurants and fast-food outlets are particularly keen on fresh-cut produce.

- Product and pricing consistency - Retailers and consumers have confidence in the fact that quality will be identical at every purchase.

Prices are also consistent, having been negotiated and set in advance, so that retailers and restaurants don't need to change prices as suppliers and quality fluctuate.

Fresh-cut products are susceptible to rapid deterioration due to the damaged cells caused during the preparation process. Therefore, packs used for such products are often modified to allow a gaseous atmosphere to develop, which slows down the ageing process. Films with widely different permeability to oxygen and carbon dioxide are available. Usually, films are much less permeable to carbon dioxide than to oxygen, so the rate of carbon dioxide accumulation is more than the corresponding rate of oxygen depletion. This atmosphere of low oxygen and increased carbon dioxide results in slowing the respiration rate of the produce, thus enhancing the shelf life.

To prepare fresh-cut salad packs on-farm, requires the purchase of refrigerated cool rooms, washing and packing facilities, bag sealing equipment and gas injection machinery. Salad leaves are washed after harvest, then dried in a spin drying machine and packed into different sized bags, with 100G packs being the most common. The bags then go through a sealing machine, which removes the air from the bag and injects a mixture of carbon dioxide and nitrogen gas, which enhances the product's shelf life. The bags themselves are often a type of modified atmosphere packaging (MAP).

Modified atmosphere packaging (MAP) results in a favourable atmosphere, which slows down the metabolic activity of the produce to a very low level and thus enables the storage of highly perishable produce for prolonged periods. The optimum modified atmosphere for lettuce salad packs is 1:1 CO_2:O_2 level.

Elevated carbon dioxide and reduced oxygen (reletive to the atmosphere) in MAP packs slows quality loss in a number of ways. The main effect is usually by suppressing respiratory activity. The lower the respiration rate of the produce, the longer its storage life, however, there are other benefits from high Carbon Dioxide and low Oxygen levels in packs, these are:

- A reduction in the production of ethylene, the plant hormone which speeds up aging and senescence;

- A reduction in rots, by directly inhibiting the growth of pathogens;

- Slower yellowing of green tissues, by preventing the break down of chlorophyll;

- Inhibition of the browning and discolouration of cut surfaces, and

- Maintenance of the food nutritional value and flavour of the product, by slowing the loss of food reserves.

Packaging Films

Films for fresh pack salads of leaf lettuce are available, which are designed to extend the storage life of the produce. Some films have special food grade additives in the film which gives the ability to control the levels of oxygen, carbon dioxide and moisture vapour in the package, while absorbing ethylene given off by the leaf tissue. Because a modified atmosphere is created, it is important to heat seal the bag.

The development and rapid growth of fresh-cut produce has been supported by technical advances. Produce shelf-life can now be extended through packing improvements, which allow produce to be seen in the plastic containers without them fogging up. There are totally controlled cool chains in the US, with shippers giving a 14 day guarantee for produce, provided the chain isn't broken. Modified atmosphere packaging is providing even greater product life. Sanitation procedures have been improved specifically for fresh-cut operations, and world class food-factory style operations have been developed. Dole, for example has spent US $75 million in the past two years on two new plants.

Total US sales of fresh produce are predicted to grow to US $94 billion by the year 2000 - a growth of more than 44% from today. Many believe that fresh-cut sales could represent 25% of the market by the turn of the century *(Anon, 1995b)*.

REFERENCES

REFERENCES

Anon, 1994(a). Cut-up vegies ready for the pot. Commercial Grower, Vol 49 no 3, April/May 1994 13 - 14.

Anon, 1994(b). Handling greenleaf. Commercial Grower, Vol 49 no 9, October/November 1994 pp23.

Anon, 1995(a). High tech and very fresh. Commercial Grower, Vol 50 no 1, Feb 1995 13 - 15.

Anon, 1995(b). Prepared vegetables product of the future. Commercial Grower, Vol 40 no 4, May 1995, 22 - 23.

Bres, W., and Weston, L. A., 1992. Nutrient accumulation and tipburn in NFT-grown lettuce at several potassium and pH levels. HortScience 27:7, 790-792.

Broadhurst, P., and Wood, R., 1996. Lettuce Ringspot. Commercial Grower, Vol 51 no 2, March 1996, 11 - 14.

Care, D., 1994. The effect of total ion concentration and flow rate on lettuce growth. Practical Hydroponics International, Issue 14, January/February 1994, 14 - 20

Cooper, A., 1996. The ABC of NFT. Casper Publications, NSW, Australia.

Cresswell, G. C., 1991. Effect of lowering nutrient solution concentration at night on leaf calcium levels and the incidence of tipburn in lettuce (var. Gloria). Journal of Plant Nutrition, 14:9 913-924.

Dalton, D., Smith, R., 1984. Hydroponic Gardening. Cobb/Horwood Publications, Auckland, New Zealand.

Economakis, C. D., 1990. Effect of solution conductivity on growth and yield of lettuce in nutrient film culture. Acta Horticulturae 287, 309 - 316.

Fisher, K. J., 1989. 'The Greenhouse Environment' in Proceedings of the Greenhouse Growers Vegetable Crops Short Course, Department of Horticultural Science, Massey University Feb 1989.

Hartmann, H. T., and Kester, D. E., 1983. Plant Propagation - Principles and Practices. Prentice/Hall International Inc, New Jersey.Jensen, M. H., and Collins, W. L., 1985. Hydroponic Vegetable Production. Horticultural Reviews, Vol 7, 483 - 554.

Kratky, B. A., 1993. A Capillary, noncirculating hydroponic method for leaf and semi-head lettuce. Horticultural Technology, April/June 1993, 206- 207.

New Zealand Agrichemical and Plant Protection Manual - 3rd Edition, 1990. Published by the NZ Agrichemical Manual Partnership, New Zealand.

Phillips, R. and Rix, M., 1993. Vegetables. Pan Books Ltd, London.

Resh, H. M., 1987. Hydroponic Food Production. Woodbridge Press Publishing Company, Santa Barbara, California.

Schwartzkopf, S. H., Dudzinski, D., and Minners, R. S., 1987. The effects of nutrient solution sterilisation on the growth and yield of hydroponically grown lettuce. HortScience, Vol 22:5, October 1987 873 - 874.

Suntec Hydroponics 1995. Nutrient Formulation Programme - Version II. Suntec Hydroponics, New Zealand.

GENERAL INDEX

GENERAL INDEX

40, 43, 46, 47, 65, 67, 70-73, 80, 90, 93, 95,
  99, 100
thermal dormancy   17
thrips   88
thyme   41
tipburn   31, 41, 72, 79, 80, 82, 83, 92-93,
  94, 95
tomatoes   52, 68, 70, 71, 73, 79, 80, 99
toxicity symptoms   78, 80

V
vacuum cooling   100
ventilation   26, 28, 71, 72, 73, 100
vermiculite   18, 20, 22, 23, 51
Verticillium lecanii   97

W
washed river sand   18
water sterilisation   68-69
water supply   25, 26, 68, 69, 82, 89
whitefly   85-87, 88, 97
wild opium   11
wilting   41, 55, 80, 83, 88, 95, 99, 100

Z
zinc   66, 75, 76, 77, 78, 79, 80, 81
zinc sulphate   81

Casper
publications

OTHER TITLES BY
CASPER PUBLICATIONS PTY LTD

The ABC of NFT by Dr Allan Cooper

Hydroponic Tomato Production by Jack Ross

The Handbook to Hydroponic Nutrient Solutions by Carl Barry

Practical Hydroponics & Greenhouses Magazine

Best of Practical Hydroponics & Greenhouses Annual

Also see our web site at:
http://www.hydroponics.com.au